Saguisag Wit – 2

Compilation of his Columns in Manila Times & other media
(Oct. 26, 2018 – Jul. 19, 2019)

By Sen. Rene Saguisag

Published IN 2019 by

TATAY JOBO ELIZES.
*Self-Publisher, under the
permission and authorization of*

RENE SAGUISAG

*author and owner of the copyright to this book. The copyright owner can
withdraw this permission at his discretion without any objection from Tatay
Jobo Elizes at any time. Printing of this book is using the present day
method of Print-On-Demand (POD) system, where prints will never run out
of copies to be available for posterity. The copyright owner is free to
republish with other publishers anytime.*

KDP ISBN

ISBN – 9781082272479
Independent Publisher

*Disclaimer: Views are expressed by the author alone. Tatay Jobo Elizes
does not knowingly publish false information and may not be held liable for
the views of the author and right to free expression.*

*Contact: job_elizes@yahoo.com
Website: http://tinyurl.com/mj76ccq
www.tatayjoboelizes.webs.com*

Published and printed in USA

Contents

1 - ATIN 'TO! - MTGIF7/19/19 – *p7*

2 - A SOCIETY IN DECAY?; PINOY VERSUS PINOY? - MTGIF7/12/19 – *p11*

3 - REALPOLITIK 101; 'BYE EKI CARDENAS' – MTGIF6/21/19 – *p15*

4 - BESSANG PASS, '45 AND A MESSAGE OF HOPE'; 75 REMEMBERED - Jun 13, 2019 – *p20*

5 - STAY AS SWEET AS YOU ARE - Jun 6, 2019 – *p25*

6 - JEWRY, DUE PROCESS 101 AND CJ RENE CORONA - MTGIF5/31/19 – *p2*

7 - JEWRY, DUE PROCESS 101 AND CJ RENE CORONA – **MTGIF5/31/19** – *p32*

8 - A PYRRHIC WIN? - TGIF5/17/19 – *p36*

9 - MY SENATE LIST; ON FOREIGN GRANTS AND FUNDS - May 9, 2019 – *p38*

10 - INDONESIA SHOWS WAY TO GO; TIMEO SERES. . . . - MTGIF5/3/19 – *p42*

11 - CALAMITOUS IRRIDENTISM AND LEBENSRAUM – MTGIF4/26/19- *p46*

12 - VOTE FOR VOICES, NOT ECHOES, IN A SCOFFLAW NATION - Apr 17, 2019 – *p52*

13 - HONESTY AND MODEST LIVES IN THE CONSTITUTION - MTGIF3/30/19 – *p56*

14 - NATIONAL MIGRAINE? - MTGIF3/23/19 – *p60*

15 - The second Fall of Bataan? - MARCH 15, 2019 – *P63*

16 - VICTOR'S JUSTICE AND SPOILS; A PROBLEM LIKE MARIA - MTGIF2/22/19 – *p68*

17 - LEI-LA PASIONARIA; MAHARLIKA? - MTGIF2-15-19 – *p72*

18 - MANNY PACQUIAO: SENATE DESAPARECIDO - MTGIF1/18/19 – *p76*

19 - NOT CHARTER, BUT CHARACTER, CHANGE - MTGIF1-4-19 – *p80*

20 - BULLY THE BULLY, RAPE THE RAPIST? - MTGIF12-28-18 – *p85*

21 - BELLS BACK WHERE THEY BELONG – MTIGIF12/14/18 – *p89*

22 - KUDOS AND THE `IGNO' PRECEDENT - MTGIF11/23/18 – *p94*

23 - SHOULD JANE RYAN BE SLAPPED PUBLICLY? NO, ABSOLUTELY! - MTGIF11-16-18 – *p99*

24 - THE 1972-86 MILITARIZATION - MTGIF11-09-18 – *p103*

25 - CREEPING MILITARIZATION NOW GALLOPING? – MTGIF11-2-18 – *p108*

26 - GOODBYE OT, RUN KOKO RUN! - MTGIF10-26-18 – *p113*

27 – *Why I publish books – Tatay Jobo Elizes – p117*

oooooo

About the Author

Rene Saguisag was born on August 14, 1939 in Mauban, Quezon, Philippines. Saguisag attended elementary school at Makati Elementary School in 1951 He graduated from Rizal High School in 1955

Saguisag went on to graduate with a Bachelor of Arts degree in 1959 from San Beda College. He also later graduated cum laude from San Beda College with a bachelor of laws degree in 1963 and placed 6th in the same year's Bar Examinations.

Saguisag also obtained his Master of Laws degree from Harvard University in 1968. Rene Saguisag practiced law as a prominent human rights lawyer in the Philippines from 1972 to 1986. He also became a spokesman for then president elect Corazon Aquino beginning on January 22, 1986. Saguisag was first elected to the Senate of the Philippines in 1987 He remained in the Senate until 1992. As a Senator, Saguisag served as chairman of the committee on ethics and privileges. He was chairman of Senate committee on ad hoc committee on the Bataan Nuclear power plant and he was one of the two senators who attended all 415 session days from July 1987 to June 1990.

Senator Saguisag worked as a checker, laborer, construction site guard and messenger from 1959 to 1962. From 1962 to 1972 he became an student researcher, then associate and eventually part time in Ledesma, Guytingco, Velasco and Saguisag. He became a member, Law Faculty (Assistant Dean 1971-1972) from 1961 to 1972. From 1972 to 1986 he practice law and a human rights lawyer. Senator Saguisag became the spokesman of candidate and president elect Cory Aquino from January 22, 1986.

He married Dulce Maramba Quintanas with whom he has four children.

Rene Saguisag practiced law as a prominent human rights lawyer in the Philippines from 1972 to 1986. He also became a spokesman for then president elect Corazon Aquinobeginning on January 22, 1986.

Rene Saguisag was one of only two Filipino Senators who attended all 415 session days from July 1987 to June 1990.[3]

Following his departure from the Senate, Saguisag became one of the leading defense lawyers in the corruption trial of former President Joseph Estrada.

Before President Estrada stepped down from Malacañang on account of the plunder case filed against him, right after the Philippine Centennial Celebration, Former Senator Rene Saguisag was appointed by Pres. Estrada to head the Ad Hoc and Independent Citizens' Committee (AHICC) with members Atty. Francis Pangilinan, Engr. Fiorello Estuar, USec. Antonio M. Llorente and Corazon dela Paz. AHICC was created by President Estrada on Feb. 24, 1999 through Administrative Order No. 53 to investigate if there were irregularities that transpired during the preparations and celebrations of Philippine Centennial Anniversary. AHICC found that the bidding for certain centennial projects had been rigged, that certain documents used in the bidding had been falsified, and that certain signatures on documents were forged.

Rene Saguisag was seriously injured in a car crash on November 8, 2007, in Makati City. A speeding dump truck struck Saguisag's van, killing his wife Dulce Saguisag, a former Secretary of the Department of Social Welfare and Development. Saguisag was left in critical condition following the collision. His injuries included seven broken ribs and small blood clots in his brain. However, his doctors stated that he had a "very good chance" of a full recovery. He spent 20 days in the intensive-care unit, and was released from the hospital on December 8, 2007.

Rene and Dulce's youngest daughter, Kaissa Saguisag is a gymnast, but a knee injury ended her quest for gold at the 24th Southeast Asian Games .[6]

Saguisag & Associates Lawyers 4045 Bigasan Street, Palanan 1235 Makati Office Nos. (+632) 551-6350/833-4140

Fax No. (+632) 831-2276. Email: ravslaw#gmail.com c/o Manila times

ooooo

1
ATIN 'TO!

MTGIF7/19/19
Manila times opinion
<opinion@manilatimes.net>

I got an invite early this week to Atin ang Pilipinas! a forum tomorrow, Saturday, on the West Philippine Sea and Sovereignty, from Pamalakaya Pilipinas. It said that "[w]hen China seized and occupied Mischief Reef in 1995, the constriction of Filipino fisherfolks' movement in their traditional fishing areas in the West Philippine Sea noticeably took its turn for the wors[e]. Fast forward to 2019, China has intensified its aggressive occupation in [our] exclusive economic zone (EEZ) in a form of reclamation intended for military build-up facilities [violating the Constitution], and harassment of Filipino fishers."

1995 was FVR's time. We don't know what Erap did in his short-lived presidency while GMA, in her long reign, was perceived to be too friendly with China {I miss her though in our fight against the restoration of the death penalty, for the abolition of which she had worked for, successfully]. Only PNoy seemed to have acted, by litigating, a civilized accepted norm for resolving disputes. I don't know if he is to blame for China's cheating on the mutual commitment to back off. Blame the victim of perfidy? Odd.

Pamalakaya continued: "The Filipino fisherfolk, who are most often front-line casualties of this long-running sea row, have been sadly enduring the Chinese military presence in their traditional fishing grounds. The recent violence was when one of China's fleets encroaching in our waters has intentionally rammed, sank, and even abandoned a Filipino fishing boat aboard 22 fishermen.

"Amid calls from the fishing sector and other patriotic sectors to actively and diplomatically assert our sovereign rights to China, the Duterte administration willfully disregards the collective clamor of the Filipino people. Its inaction on the issue is highly prevalent[?] and it even verbally [I'd say ORALLY, as `verbal' covers both the spoken and written word] allows China to exploit our waters with all their might, at the expense of the Filipino fisherfolk.

"It is in this light that we will be having a Public Forum entitled `Atin ang Pilipinas': a forum on West Philippine Sea and Sovereignty' on July 20, 2019, Saturday, 3:00-5:00 pm [tomorrow], at UP Diliman College of Mass Communication Auditorium."

The invite is signed by Fernando "Ka Pando" Hicap, National Chairperson.

Thank you very very many, haha, Ka Pando, but, regrets, I need to be in a faculty meet and my class in San Beda where I'll touch on our unfortunate policy of seeming appeasement.

The encroachment may have started during FVR's time, per Pamalakaya, a group of fishermen who should know what they are talking about. FVR, Erap and GMA arguably apparently did nothing.(?) PNoy decided to sue and won. Now, he's being blamed. Weird.

There's nothing to be gained though in blaming past Presidents. More relevant than playing the Blame Game is what the incumbent is going to do about an inherited problem with a greedy neighbor. The hitch is he says "wala naman tayong maggagawa." He now admits having reached an oral - again, not "verbal," which includes oral and written - agreement with Xi in 2016 and which we learned about only recently. What gave the Prez the right secretly to give away to, or share, our patrimony, with, China? He cannot secretly give orally to a foreign counterpart the right to exploit our natural resources, such as access to our rich fishing grounds, and tell us only years later about it. It took a merciless ramming incident for the public to know a secret love, as it were.

We know of Prez Woodrow Wilson's famous 1918 14 Points, with No. 1 dealing with "open covenants openly arrived at after which there shall be no private international understandings of any kind. . . ." Certainly not, when exploitation of our natural resources is involved, among other things. The people, through the elected Senate, must be involved in a hearing where our fishermen could be heard for the benefit of the Emperor from Davao.. The fishing grounds belong to us, not the Prez's private fiefdom. He has to care for Luzon fisherfolk.

"Private international understandings of any kind"? Would it cover horny Trump and Putin hiring prostitutes? Indonesia's Soekarno supposedly arranged the purchase of a Forbes Park mansion for mistress Amelia Amante de la Rama, who he would marry later. Again, my fraternal advice, in excursus, "Mr. Prez, marry na si Honeylet if only for appearances in diplomatic functions. It is the right thing to do."

If he finally goes to the U.S. - he now after all says in effect that he also cares for the millions of Pinoys there who may be nuked if his irresponsible taunt to fire the first shot is followed by the U.S. - he can be accompanied in official functions by Honeylet. The other kulasisis left behind can only eat their hearts out, and settle for postcards. Trump, facing many lurid allegations, may not mind, but decent old-fashioned Americans may.

I love people who interfere on behalf of our human rights victims. It is the UNIVERSAL, not the PAROCHIAL, Declaration of Human Rights, after all. It delights us in our small insignificant human rights community concerned about innocent children being victimized in our insane bloody messy and failed anti-poor drug war.

Alien interference encourages us, hearing about a salvaged child or a peasant's daughter raped by a son of the hacendero. The victims' kin soon realize that the law represents the biases of the ruling class, and go to Tondo or the NPA for redress. Victims of injustice go there as an NPA trooper may be a rebel with a cause, an unredressed grievance, or to foreign fora, such as the UN, whose Declaration of 1948 we had played key role in its proclamation. Not PAROCHIAL, but UNIVERSAL. December 10, I, as a student of human rights, remember as the anniversary of the proclamation of the Universal [not Parochial] Declaration of Human Rights, in 1948, in Paris [also the venue when Spain ceded us to the U.S., for $20M on the same date in 1898, in the Treaty of Paris].

When Assistant Secretary of State Patt Derian was sent here by Prez Jimmy Carter, she walked out of a dinner with the Marcoses, to visit Ninoy Aquino. Macoy's administration tried to make a non-chivalrous play on words on Derian as Durian. Patt and Jimmy interfered here and in Argentina, etc., hallelujah. Patt, Jimmy had sought not for her diplomatic experience or skills but her "moral fiber", seemingly in very short supply in this braggadocio narcissistic administration. I am reminded of Balzac's epigram: behind every great wealth is a great crime.

The panic and terror at being probed arguably indicates a guilty conscience. The administration isn't able to say, "sure, you're welcome? What else can we do for you?" This casual response may be Iceland's in case there's a hue and cry for tit for tat: probe Iceland's possible human rights abuses. Any Pinoys there complaining? They won't benefit from a > diplomatic cut-off, as suggested by Senator Imee, a human rights violator in the salvaging of Archimedes Trajano, judicially established.

Thousands have been killed by Pulis Patolas playing god, deciding who will live and who will die. Bato de la Rosa now again childishly offers to be decapitated. Ano na po ba ang nangyari sa Senado natin? May laman po ba ang mga ulo duon ng ilan at ginagamit po ba ang kukote? In this regard, we hope and pray neither Manny Pacquiao nor Keith Thurman gets hurt badly on Sunday, such as being brain-damaged by repeated blows to the head in the manly art of modified murder - W.O. McGeehan.

Why has the current administration made some of us feel that we are back in the 70's? Brain-damaged? Is Senator Leila de Lima being detained insensately the way Ninoy

Aquino, Pepe Diokno, and many others were, beginning on September 22, 1972, midnight?

The other night, I heard the Tennessee Waltz and Blue Bayou sang beautifully, the kind of trip down memory lane I enjoy. But, not having to use tabo again in bathing, which I did not have to prior to June 30, 2016. Tttuuubbbiiggg! And a week ago, from our Palanan home to Makati Med, two hours; before that date, 15 minutes, max. What's happening to the quality of our lives?

And then ATIN 'TO, we are giving away.

Please try tomorrow to be in UP, whose cagers and alums memorably popularized the fighting chant late last year in the UAAP.

Saguisag & Associates Lawyers 4045 Bigasan Street, Palanan 1235 Makati Office Nos. (+632) 551-6350/833-4140 Fax No. (+632) 831-2276

oooooo

2
A SOCIETY IN DECAY?; PINOY VERSUS PINOY?

Manila times opinion
<opinion@manilatimes.net>
MTGIF7/12/19

The Speaker is No. 4 in the line of succession to the presidency. Indeed, certain of the Speakers we have had arguably been of presidential timber quality. That some of the aspirants to be No. 4 we had just read about belonged to the Lapiang Pinabili Lang ng Suka or the Wassiname or Whosis Party again indicated the state of our putrefaction in a society in decay. Household names only in their own households. For No. 4, for crying out loud!

The Prez was saying he would not interfere; then he proceeds to inflict his will, via a discombobulating term-sharing deal that makes eunuchs of the House, whose right to decide on who would lead it, it abandoned, sans any struggle, resistance and whimper.

A truly independent House worthy of respect can change leaders any time, on its own. The administration has yet to understand the virtue of subtlety. Whatever Lolo D wants, Lolo gets, while everyone focuses on a committee to head and its budget, fantasizing on being addressed Mr. or Madame Chair, preening before TV cameras.

But, we do have to give Speakers Alan Peter Cayetano (a fait accompli) and Allan Lord Velasco (a dream, even a fantasy, a lot can happen in 15 months; when politicians shake hands, they should count their fingers afterwards). Their term-share may be questionable as despicable trafficking in public office. But, let's see what they can do to give our people mired in massive poverty a better life.

Serious traffic problems. No urban planning. Just Build!Build! Build! Bahala na po. Last urban lungs going, going, gone. Poor commuters lining up in the dead of night, in the wind and rain. No water or in trickles. Massive vote-buying. Countless homeless. Many crooks and gross human rights violators in office. Good officials named, shamed and deep-sixed sans due process. Proud and profane high officials with limited vocabulary cuss. A judicial system without predictability - but I do appreciate the High Court's recent reported decision, via ponente Justice Diosdado Peralta, favoring prisoners, which should help decongest our overcrowded jails, etc.. Prominently publicized, but we cannot, as of the other day, get a copy of a decision in a case I assisted an idealistic human rights neophyte.

Are we now a society in decay? Following savagery and civilization? Now our patrimony and sovereignty are in jeopardy.

No matter who was to blame for the June 9 maritime incident, the Chinese should not have abandoned our 22 fishermen nor lied about supposedly swarming uncaring Pinoy vessels. The criminal abandonment reinforces the theory that the Chinese vessel is part of China's maritime militia and its crew feared being found out, scaring our probers, if any, who had to find fault in the 22, to appease and not displease China.

When we, per our Constitution, renounced war as an instrument of national policy, we meant, I think, a paradigm for all. Else, in the classic statement of Senator Bato de la Rosa, "shit happens." That he misspoke reinforces the belief that military intelligence could be a contradiction in terms. In the end, Bato sorta apologized kuno, rare in our arrogant palalo o hambog culture.

But, why should our proud and profane Prez taunt Trump to go to war with China by taking the first shot when Trump is busy making friends with North Korea? Warmongering is not in our culture or Constitution. If astig Kanto Boy Digong gets the elephANTS to quarrel - with his childish taunt, "my Kuya Xi can beat you, Tito Sam" - what about us, ANTS? A stray missile may wipe out Metro Manila. Cebu and Davao. And risk pitting Pinoy versus Pinoy as will be shown below.

Digong should not be a soltador in a cockpit inducing the U.S. and China to make sabong. I grew up in a sabong culture, in Mauban (a late Uncle was fond of it) and Pasig (my late Kuya was). There, I heard kristo, tiyope, tupada, bulik, alimbyugin, llamado, dehado, pakahig, tari, rueda, pintakasi, lodies, rerebe, himas. atbp.. I hear of Pinoy-sponsored tupadas in the U.S., where Macoy, na-tiyope, fled to in 1986. (In a televised 1986 debate with Caballero Tsikboy Ka Turing Tolentino, when he said gently that I had no proof that candidate Cory, my principal had won, I said, "kayo naman po, Ka Turing, ang tandang na na-tiyope at tumalilis, talo ng inahin").

Pinoys who escaped from Mexico and its galleons, and settled in Louisiana, just might have introduced sabong to the natives. There was supposed to be a Pinoy enclave. A book on chess genius Paul Morphy I read long ago said there were Filipinos - so-called even centuries ago in New Orleans. The Manila Men introduced dried shrimps in the bayous and married blacks, Creoles and other minorities, but not Caucasians or WASPs (White Anglo-Saxon Protestants). Forbidden.

Too bad, the Pinoy settlements in their tiny corner of the world have been obliterated by hurricanes.

If China and U.S. openly quarrel violently, not only would the world tremble. That may be how the world as we know it would crumble and end.

It could test the loyalty of Pinoy migrants in the U.S.. The Manila Men of 1812 fought with Jean Lafitte and General Andrew "Old Hickory" Jackson (the 7th U.S. Prez) against the Brits in the decisive Battle of New Orleans of January 8, 1815. Outnumbered, but not outfought. If Digong leads us into a war between China and the U.S. and chooses to side with the former, we might be fighting our own people in America. Pinoy versus Pinoy. That is why before he opens his mouth, Digong should think matters through and their consequences.

There are millions of Pinoys in the U.S. Digong's taunt just might lead to war which no one could win, and annihilate everything. Only two apes may survive and grouse that they have to start all over again.

But, seriously, back to the here and now, on term limits, can one really have enough of a Lorenzo M. Tañada, Sr. or a Jovito R. Salonga by reading out "consecutive&q uot; in the Constitution? I could only basically look at pages 90 and 91 of the August 1, 1986 proceedings of the Constitutional Commission Record, so thick and heavy I could hardly use it without risking a slipped disc. Did I cherry-pick from the 1,587 pages of my two volumes? For now, I believe we should not read out "consecutive" and the rest period is three years, as articulated by Commissioner Chito Gascon; no one disagreed. We should not throw away the priceless extra of experience of a Recto, Laurel, Salonga, Tolentino, Diokno, Padilla, Rodrigo, et al., in favor of those who still have to look for the comfort room.

But, looking at the House and Senate now, one might wish "no term" at all sana for some.

Finally, I found last Tuesday a Daily Tribune headline I could agree with: "Cayetano, Velasco Halve Speakership - Rody caves in to `sharing' ." I was reminded of cavemen and their best thinking in a jurassic era.

Let us see. Alan and Allan, yes, Godspeed, show us what you can do to give our people a better life, while Sal Panelo contorts himself into a pretzel.

And no, we cannot have a second Fil-Am War. On February 4, 1898, Private William Grayson of the Nebraska Volunteers fired the first shot in Sociego St., in Sta. Mesa (in Manila, not San Juan). Englishman Grayson was doing sentry duty, and encountered three Filipino soldiers ("niggers, " to him, a racist). The victim was Cpl. Anastacio Felix of the 4th Company, Morong Battalion.

No! to a second Fil-Am War! The Prez should unite, not divide, us.

And grave reservations I have, I regret to have to say, on widely-admired Amal Clooney, not just another pretty face, getting aboard for iconic Maria Ressa. FLAG and Teddy Te can do the job. I don't relish the thought of Tanny, Pepe and Joker spinning in their graves. In our time, we had to rely on ourselves in dealing with Macoy, Chief Justice (CJ) Iking Fernando and SolGen Titong Mendoza. CJ Iking was said to look down on non-UP law alums as a lower form of animal life, but I managed to weather his toughest questions and came out in one piece, I like to think, in my first oral argument in the Supreme Court in 1982.

I don't want Digong meddling in the House leadership. And it is enough, from where I sit, for Amal to express her solidarity but the nitty-gritty is for formidable Teddy to handle. Kaya po ni Teddy yan.

But, is our judiciary not in decay also? As the poets sing, if we are all in the gutter, in decay, some of us must keep looking at the stars. And our reach should exceed our grasp, or what's a heaven for?

Saguisag & Associates Lawyers 4045 Bigasan Street, Palanan 1235 Makati Office Nos. (+632) 551-6350/833-4140 Fax No. (+632) 831-2276

oooooo

3
REALPOLITIK 101; 'BYE EKI CARDENAS'

Manila times opinion - opinion@manilatimes.net
MTGIF6/21/19

Realpolitik Lesson No. 1: The U.S. military, or anybody else's military, would come to help us if it would be in its interests to do so. Again, Kissinger, to whom is attributed - a country has no permanent friends or enemies, only permanent interests. Echoing Lord Palmerston, who said no eternal allies, no perpetual enemies, only interests are eternal and perpetual. (Kissinger deserves to be known not only for saying that power is the ultimate aphrodisiac. Power can make one gwaping, is one reading of it. Who are in power today?)

We were one huge military base of the U.S. in 1941; it was in its interests to thwart Japan's invasion. No dice though as we were occupied and trampled upon anyway. But, the U.S. would come to help if it would be in its best interests to do so, treaty or no.. Same with other countries. Same guiding star that led us to side with China against Japan in WWII, lack of treaty nowithstanding.

And then, there is the UN, and Rome. Digong should not be so defeatist.

The Chinese dragon cannot just swat us as a dragonfly. I am just sorry I am leaving it to my children and apos to fight the Asian Goliath, if it comes to that. Approaching 80, and needing a cane on uneven surface, I may just shoot myself in the foot and become a wheelchair case. But, what war? We simply want China to do the right thing by taking responsibility, restitute, and not lie about Pinoys swarming all over the place where F/B GM VIR1 was anchored, immobile, and destroyed. But utterly.

If the Chinese could lie on the alleged swarming, they could on all else. Falsus in uno, falsus in omnibus, with which non-lawyers may not be familiar. Like civilian Cabinet members who may even conclude that the alleged Pinoy swarm attacked the innocent Chinese. So, enough already, Sec. Manny Piñol. But, bravo, Sec. Delfin Lorenzana for asking for an apology, etc.. What about their Boss?

For some reason, I recall Aixa telling exiled son Boadbil, in the mountain crag from which he turned around and wept at the last sighting of the beloved Granada he had lost, without a fight, in 1492 - "you would do well to weep like a woman, for the loss of a kingdom you could not defend as a man." The site is now known as El Ultimo Suspiro del Moro, The Last Sigh of the Moor. Digong should not visit her admirable Nanay Soling's grave and again weep, at risk of being Boadbilled.

Digong should meet the rammed fishermen, hear their sighs, and ask them whether there were indeed seven and eight boats of Pinoy fishermen who were around and did nothing - I am incredulous - to help the F/B GM VIR1 crew. Fake news from Beijing? *Tayo pa ang pinalalabas na mga bugoy, kuyog, na bubugbugin sila?* It had to be fellow fishermen from Vietnam who came to the rescue, doing the decent humane thing, or else it would not only have been the vessel that would have been literally dead in the water.

The Vietnamese, fewer than Pinoys, beat France, the U.S. and China. (In Monterey recently, the family went to a Vietnamese resto, no Pinoy counterpart where my apos could have their fave sinigang. Divine Meryl Streep followed us in Monterey but she was a week late. Sorry about that.) PUSO makes the difference. The Vietnamese have it.

Digong is uncharacteristically not in the mood for a Fire!Aim!Ready! response, on China. But, Ready!Aim!Fire! is really for everyone, not only for China. It is presidential not to prejudge. So, let the probers talk with the fishermen and not mind the Prez's unrequited fondness for, or fear of, China.

Digong may be our most quarrelsome Prez ever but when it comes to China, "wait a minute. . . ." How will the Cabinet probers read him? *Matatameme*. A directive to tuck their tails between their legs? Would they shame him by saying that it was not a "little maritime accident" but deliberate big-time bullying? A no-brainer. Echoes, not voices, the probers are.

In 1991, weary of foreign interloping, I helped vote to end the uninterrupted presence of foreign troops on our soil for centuries. And non, je ne regrette rien. No, I regret nothing. Foreign intrusion can come in many forms, even on agreement. Any arm's length deal now following the constitutional procedure is fine by me. The people should be heard, through a referendum, or the Senate, which PNoy and his Cabinet bypassed in the 2013 EDCA (Enhanced Cooperation Defense Agreement). An unrepentant Supreme Court (SC) did not correct the Constitutional cavaliers.

Constitutional overreach we had in 2001 when the SC ruled that Erap had resigned. He was the last one to know he had done so pala. Among those adversely affected was Deputy Executive Secretary Ramon "Eki" Cardenas, as efficient a public servant as one could find. Last Sunday, gone. His departure I learned from Cora S. de la Paz-Bernardo my fellow Rizal Hi alum. She and Eki attended Cornell at the same time.

In 2003, Eki was charged in connection with the Oakwood caper, where government double-crossed Sonny Trillanes & Co., a bitter disappointment the redoubtable Max Soliven carried to his grave. Now, as to Sonny, the administration is again rattling the bones of a skeleton from which all semblance of life has long departed. Bullies.

One July 2003 night, Eki called to say he was being arrested. From a family dinner out in Heritage, I rushed to his place. He and I were made to board the same car, bound for Camp Crame. And a cop with us, riding shotgun, later testified that he had overheard us talk in incriminating terms. A lawyer's instinct is to advise a client to exercise his right not to speak, to remain silent and not commit suicide. Such stark police perfidy is one reason I urge not to accord our pulis patolas the presumption of regularity in the performance of official functions. They have not earned it. Too many stories of operations by composite teams with a member from the Bureau of PLANT Industry.

Judge Oscar B. Pimentel lifted from, say, my quaint paper, where I had written: "We have the cockamamie story that some woman took out garbage which serendipitously provided evidence, thereby insulting our little intelligence. Who was this mystery woman in his gated community coming out of the house that was vacant? And was not to be found again because the pulis patola incredibly allegedly left no one in the premises or the vicinity of the same in the few intervening hours before the fateful raid." Order, Jan. 17, 2008, page 6.

Judge Pimentel must have known that one visiting someone in an exclusive plutocratic enclave, cannot just walk in the park, as it were. There would be phone calls exchanged. A mystery woman who was never identified, much less investigated? Thus, the Judge ruled - ". . . , finding the demurrer to evidence meritorious with respect to lack of sufficient evidence to require the accused to present his evidence, the Demurrer to Evidence is GRANTED, and as a consequence, the case is hereby dismissed. . . ." At page 20.

Fellow Atenean Vic Barrios says Eki followed his footsteps in Cornell, in everything, save as Tinikling dancer.

In another promulgation last Friday afternoon, Acting Parañaque RTC Judge Betlee-Ian J. Barraquias acquitted a son of Sen. Ramon Revilla, Sr. (who must be exhausted responding to Happy Father's Day greetings from his many bunga ng pagmamahalan) . There I played but a cameo role, the real workhorses being Compañeros Jeffrey Gepte and Fred Perito. When the Judge graciously noted my presence and asked why I was not standing to be recognized, I said, "thank you, Your Honor, pero taga-abot lang po ako ng folder dito." All the accused were acquitted and the courtroom exploded, reminiscent in a very small way of the manner the Raptors did hours earlier in knocking off the Golden State Warriors. Tears of relief and joy, after years in jail.

In the 5th game of the 2019 NBA Finals, Walking

Wounded Kevin Durant played briefly and the inspired Warriors won. I recalled Willis Reed's cameo appearance in the 7th game between the Knicks and the Lakers on May 8, 1970. He sank two quick jumpers and returned to the bench quickly but inspired the team enough to get the whole enchilada.

We need the Prez to inspire us, in a game that may be for all the marbles. Aixa's reproof reverberates across the centuries. You would do well to weep for the loss of water (tttuuubbbiiiggg!) and dignity (if our fishermen' s anchored vessel was indeed rammed and those aboard, abandoned) you could not defend as a man.

But, let us accord the Prez the due process he denies others. Again, his failure is yours and mine, his success, yours and mine, too. No expletive for Xi Jinping? Very good. He must really avoid the blunt tool of invective, adding heat, not light, and address issues as calmly as he can.

Saguisag & Associates Lawyers 4045 Bigasan Street, Palanan 1235 Makati Office Nos. (+632) 551-6350/833- 4140 Fax No. (+632) 831-2276

oooooo

4

BESSANG PASS, '45 AND 'A MESSAGE OF HOPE'; 75 REMEMBERED

Jun 13, 2019 <ravslaw@gmail.com>

Let us recall this weekend our glorious June 14-15, 1945 victory at Bessang Pass. The Great Pretender, Marcos, claimed credit for it that should go to Conrado Rigor, Sr., Desi

Jurado, Russell Volckmann, and many others who were there. Macoy was the man who never was, not even for a second. Tibo Mijares wrote in The Conjugal Dictatorship that Macoy was busy in buy-and-sell during WWII while his Ma was selling drugs to high school studes, and arrested by Detective Telesforo Tenorio (later chief of Manila's Finest). Pp. 393-94 (rev. and ann. ed. 2017).

While we should not forget nor even downplay the April 9, 1942 Fall of Bataan commemoration - Good Losers we are - I submit that our glorious 1945 Ascension in Bessang Pass should not just be relegated to a footnote.

We cherish our Mactan, Balangiga and Bessang Pass memories. Next year will mark the 75th Bessang Pass Anniversary of what led to Yamashita' s capture. We lost nearly a thousand men in the semester-long campaign. Volckmann remained, while McArthur left in 1942, and vowed to return, which he did, in 1944. June 14-15, 2020 should be celebrated the way the Allies marked last June 6, the day in 1944 they landed in Normandy, to start the final push against Hitler; his patented fist bump, the Nazi salute, Duterte insensitively copies and asks his guests to do with him, mocking the suffering of the vilified and persecuted Jews Prez Quezon correctly welcomed.

In the late 70's or early 80's, I bumped into Desi, a fellow teacher in San Beda who dazzled with his mastery of civil law (and later became a Court of Appeals Justice). He said he admired the way we kept the human rights torch burning. And then, with that faraway look, wondered whatever happened to that young man who decades earlier was ready to give his all for the Motherland. That I read to mean, "keep going," and we, ever so few, did. We could use the encouragement of the vets, like Desi and Uncle Jovy Salonga, tortured by the Japanese.

In October 1975, Uncle issued a message for us not to lose our moral stamina. I unhesitatingly signed it (while editing the Rizal IBP Newsletter, which I was told Justice JBL Reyes characterized as the only free paper at the time), and joined in its distribution along with Joe Balajadia, Raul Pangalangan, et al.. Uncle wrote:

"On October 10, 1975, a representative group of more

than 150 citizens, led by Father Horacio de la Costa [my fellow Maubanin] and myself, issued a 75-page pamphlet, titled `A Message of Hope to Filipinos Who Care.' It contained an analysis of three years of martial law, an evaluation of the New Society, a projection of the future, and a proposed alternative. Despite the repressive measures imposed under martial law, we published the following appeal:

"We believe that when a system becomes so unjust and oppressive that more and more people are minded to resist its commands, a deliberate and public refusal to obey becomes a supreme act of conscience. A nonviolent system of noncooperation, adequately carried out at the proper time, can render the ways of violence unnecessary. As long as peaceful methods of resistance to injustice and oppression are effective, we shall avail [ourselves] of them. . . ." A Journey of Struggle & Hope 240-41 (2001).

1975 saw few critics of Martial Law (ML) on its third year; I'd be advised by well-meaning kith and kin to give up my anti-ML obsession. "Anong mangyayari sa pamilya mo, kung makulong o mapatay ka?" That is why if we merited a little bit of recognition, it should also be a tribute to our spouses taking care of our innocent kids when we could not bring up the bread in our pro bono or puro abono practice, of abonados, not abogados.

Let us remember today the rousing victory in Bessang Pass and not to forget the many ordinary Filipinos who helped the Rigors, Jurados, Bañezes and Volckmanns make it happen. Now, again our democracy seems to be in ICU. Principal triumph over Principle last May 13, it seemed. Echoes, not Voices, we don't need in what we called the Better House, to tell it apart from the Bigger House, on which we may have to give up. Pera-pera po duon according to former Speaker Bebot Alvarez. Disgraceful.

The Prez even orders the arrest of people, with no preliminary investigation, a power Macoy shared with JPE for years, and now reportedly asserted even by Energy Secretary Alfonso Cusi. And the Executive Secretary, Justice Secretary, Legal Counsel, the Integrated Bar, Philconsa, et al., appear to look the other way. Either in silence, or even in support. Along with the Senate, which it seems to me, is not for everyone. The institution of Don Claro and Amang should attract those who will toil, and not treat policy-making and lawmaking as hobbies, diversions or sidelines, while focused on the money and press coverage their principal activity will bring. No more dedicated Claro Rectos and Amang Rodriguezes? Kapakanang pambayan po sana, di po pangsarili. There is no report about jockeying to chair some ethics committee, gone extinct(?) at a time when propriety may have become a desaparecido.

Have the wells of patriotism and public service really run dry? Have we lost our moral stamina?

The militarization of the civil service for instance should stop. DSWD (Department of Social Work and Development) Secretary Rolando Bautista, whose military credentials for the post are suspect, must learn to thrive in a hardy climate, and take the rough with the smooth. It is not easy for a Pinoy to apologize (routine elsewhere); he should have been tolerant and sporting towards civilian Erwin Tulfo. If the General cannot take the heat, he should get out of the kitchen, and return the post to a civilian social worker. Or sue Erwin for libel but the Supreme Court may only maintain a nominal fine imposed by a trial court, if that. The outrageous demand for a donation of humongous sums to various charities simply discombobulates. The press must take a stand against militaristic irridentism. Ang yayabang po ng mga Tulfo, pero ang militar, mga palalo! Ang mayabang, galit daw po sa kapwa mayabang. Such arrogance of power, inspired by our most quarrelsome Prez ever.

2019 is like Macoy's 1975, when the civilian populace dreaded the military. And Macoy, by himself, could then order the arrest of anyone. What's this we hear about Digong ordering the arrest of the owners of a dialysis center? Without any preliminary investigation? Are we under undeclared martial law? Are the government lawyers asleep? Now, as abovementioned, this shocking head: "Cusi orders shooters' arrest." He may not even be a lawyer like JPE.

When will they ever learn?

Thus, to migrate to the U.S. for breathing space is the

dream of many desperate Pinoys. When we (my youngest son, daughter and apo) applied for US visas last May 23, for a June 1 wedding in Monterey, Ca., the queue that morning was long. Now I read that it is sorta downgrading its services. I am content with my dual citizenship, Pinoy and Senior, but do not begrudge our countless citizens wanting to migrate there or even fantasizing that we become its 51st state. Hell, no! But, for all its negatives, for one thing, the U.S. has helped steady the price of oil, with its vast reserves, now said to be larger than those of the rest of the world combined.

In Monterey for less than a week (May 29 to June 4), I appreciated not seeing a single two-storey building in contrast to our wild build!build! build! frenzy, helping cut or reduce our water supply here in Palanan, Makati. High-rises do not provide garden space. Do we have any urban planners at all at a time when our few lungs or green space are being devoured by the avaricious builders? We had water on June 30, 2016.. Now, it is like a firefly. Count me among those unhappy and unsatisfied after three years. Tuuuubbbiiiggg!

Our human rights continue to depreciate. And to think that we were a prime mover behind the Universal Declaration of Human Rights. We were glad when Jimmy Carter meddled in our human rights situation. But, the administration keeps reading Universal as Parochial Or Insular. It can use a dictionary.

Even parochially, we see the Prez relocating the domestic airport to Sangley. Nothing from Congress which hears out the people to cross-fertilize ideas. How much will it cost? I read P552.02B! Who has the power of the purse anyway? Who conducts hearings on appropriation, environental impact, access by road and sea, and asks foolish questions? Is water adequate? Or will Caviteños share our misery?

Tttuuubbbiiiggg?

But, the Prez says Makati to Cubao in minutes. The difficult Digong and Art Tugade can do right away, the impossible takes a little longer.. Who can say, "Mr. President, wait a minute. . . ?"

Saguisag & Associates Lawyers 4045 Bigasan Street, Palanan 1235 Makati> Office Nos. (+632) 551-6350/833- 4140 Fax No. (+632) 831-2276

oooooo

5
STAY AS SWEET AS YOU ARE

Jun 6, 2019 <ravslaw@gmail..com>

Condolences to those left behind by Gary Lising, 78, whose risible tales we lauded, and Teddy Regala, 85, whose exquisite mastery of American major league baseball awed me.

I left this piece in rough draft form against the possibility that I may be under the weather on getting home after a very brief visit to the U.S. for a wedding (not mine, ha, that of a daughter who has just won another literary prize, and not to watch Toronto make taranta Golden State, in the NBA Finals first game, either; in gentrified Monterey, smooth disciplined traffic, no two-storey building I can recall, plenty of water, no talk of high office being bought, unlike our polls and the speakership, etc., reasons enough to be "happy" and "satisfied". There, the land of the brave and the home of the free (could be, the land of the bribe and the home of the fee), as I read again Mario Puzo's Godfather, where I re-read that a lawyer with a briefcase can steal more money than a thousand men with guns and mask. We may have too many of this sordid type and don't need more shysters.

More than once in the past, I have used in the main the core of what appears below - here, kinda updated - to salute our new lawyers, with a caveat.** May I felicitate the new lawyers due to take their oaths on Monday afternoon, at three,

June 13, at the PICC, thusly, below (while appreciating Otso Diretso' s Erin Tañada's Christian advice to the unlucky ones: never give up; indeed, my friends, we are never given crosses heavier than we can bear):

"Compañeros/ as, I see that 1,800 of you, 2018 examinees, passed last year's bar examinations and will now take your oath.

"Now you feel being on top of the world basking in the many-splendored afterglow of a well-earned achievement. There will be many big nights on the town, but the mornings after inevitably bring the cold light of day, so to say.

"What else can one say to you after welcoming you to the guild and expressing the ritualistic good wishes? Where will you be years from now? Particularly the superior ones?

"The driving dream that lifted many of you in your school days was that the law offers, a good, if not the best, way of serving the poor, obscure and oppressed, the unwashed mob, the least of our brethren, as it were, to attain a measure of justice. Too often however, it takes only a few years of practice plus a taste of the good life for this consuming passion to sink without a trace in the deep rugs of a well-appointed law office, amid the staccato clatter of top-of-the-line thingamajigs and the hum of multi-horse-powered air-conditioners.

"Co-optation was the word for it in the language of the street-wise radicals of past years. Moral stamina is a precious jewel.

"Who among you, unpublicized and unadvertised, away from microphones and cameras, will quietly advocate the causes of the poor or unpopular, condemned by the lynch mob? Not for the experience either but to be true to a promise to try to fight the manipulators and the oppressors in society. *"Mga naghaharing uri"*, we used to cry, even as we note that the law represents the biases of the ruling classes in their plutocratic enclaves.

"Some of you, feeling your word is your bond, will possibly stick it out for a while. But, probably, not many. Somewhere down the road, the thought of your kids going around barefooted, of not going to expensive elitist schools,

26

and of you being labelled unsuccessful for not being affluent, will stare you in the face and bite deeply into your psyche. And then you will kiss a dream goodbye to join those who defend the rich and the powerful with ruthless efficiency.

"In the process you will strengthen, willy-nilly, your clients' near monopolistic stranglehold on the country' s finest talents, aggravating the imbalance in the power situation in society. Mediocrities can go far in our society but it is the loss of the bright ones - who know the law, not the judge - that really hurts.

"Holmes once said that happiness does not come from material rewards. `[H]appiness, ' he wrote, `I am sure from having known many successful men, cannot be won simply by being counsel for great corporations and having an income of fifty thousand dollars.' Oh, yeah? To celebrate cynicism, may very well be the response or retort of the hired guns retained by the oligarchs, particularly those who had their positions buttressed and reinforced with the installation of today's quasi-martial law apparatus in a seeming police state reinforced by militarization of the bureaucracy. How naive could Holmes get?

"Still and all, we are delighted to welcome you, the new lawyers, to the fraternity (and sorority). Do achieve, and acquire what you will, but - never ever forget the least. lost and last: the psychic income is something not all the money in the world can buy.

"Do consider human rights lawyering. Fight the anti-poor drug campaign - the drug lords and their protectors laugh their way to the bank, as it were - and the anti-poor death penalty."

Reflect on the last elections. Have we just witnessed the suicide of democracy, validating John Adams' view: "There never was a democracy yet that did not commit suicide"?

That our hopelessly profane Prez expects guests to imitate him in brandishing the Nazi salute is ominous. So we echo Harvard Professor Annette Gordon-Reed's concern: "Are we in danger of undermining our democracy? [Thomas] Jefferson understood that we need an educated and involved electorate to protect democracy. She also pointed out the danger of too much money in politics, and said this is something that the Framers did not anticipate." One Senator-elect's statement of contributions and expenses (SOCE) should be interesting, given the remarkably extravagant campaign by his camp, from where I sit. Nothing like it I have seen before. A tsunami of unseemly political advertising.

So, Compañeros/ras stay as sweet as you are.

To thine own self be true. Follow the fixed stars pointed out to you by the Rectos, role models of whom we cannot have enough, Uncle Jovy Salonga topped the Senate race thrice. Do we throw away the priceless extra of experience?

That you and I may never cease to dream.

Saguisag & Associates Lawyers4045 Bigasan Street, Palanan1235 MakatiOffice Nos. (+632) 551-6350/833- 4140 Fax No. (+632) 831-2276*

oooooo

6
JEWRY, DUE PROCESS 101 AND CJ RENE CORONA

MTGIF5/31/19 - Manila times opinion <opinion@manilatimes.net>

When this piece comes out, I'd most likely be in the U.S., despite my health issues, to be there on June 1. There, and then, my daughter Lara is getting wed. Any father would like to make such a day perfect, to the extent that he would have anything to do with it. This trip is also what her late sainted mother would have wanted to be taken by me, a Super-Takusa (meaning one who loved her, with that kind of passion what whips the blood,and always will).

Our visas were granted only last May 23. We had been booked to fly out the other night. Our visa interview had originally been set on July 2. I had to use my tremendous influence with one who looked like our Foreign Affairs Secretary, to advance the interview. Done. Thank you very many, haha, Pareng Ted and Mareng Louie Locsin. So, off to the wedding, to reconnect with kith and kin, made possible by the DFA's and the Embassy's kindness, right after my own heart.

It also warmed my heart to see Amazing Grace Poe and Nancy With the Laughing Face Binay, in their proclamation not thrusting their clenched right fist forward, criminal in nations trampled upon by Hitler. The Nazi right fist-bump Aussie Spymaster Nick Warner got hammered, pummelled and pilloried from pillar to post for, after aping Digong naively in the Palace in August 2017.

Another woman with balls, veteran diplomat Delia Albert, had alsodeclined to join the foolish disparagement.

Aging and ailing like me, Digong, six years younger than I, may not have the strength to raise his right hand above the Hitler level. But Dr. Sal Panelo tells us not to worry. Reassuring?

But, really, we should be more sensitive to the sensibilities of the Jewry. 6,000,000 Jews were massacred by Hitler (Digong halved it to 3,000,000 in 2016). We credit Prez Quezon for admitting members of one of the most vilified and persecuted minorities in history. The refugees were fleeing from the Holocaust before World War II.

Our Prez took an oath to do justice to everyone. Instead of convicting anyone by publicity, why not file charges and prove same? Like in the case of the poor Food and Drug Administration chief.

When Nixon blasted Charles Manson for the killing of actress Sharon Tate, criticism was swift and strong; Nixon immediately retreated. Yup, our Prez-elect vows to do justice to everyone. It is not his place to prejudge the guilt or innocence of anyone. For him to adjudge anyone innocent or guilty puts undue pressure on the prosecution, judiciary and witnesses not to embarrass him.

How many have been condemned by Digong, from critics to alleged narco-politicians? He should review our Bill of Rights and the Universal Declaration of Human Rights. We lament the spectacle of judges inhibiting themselves in sensitive widely-publicized cases maybe so as not to risk offending the appointing and promoting power.

We must reintroduce Digong to due process as he nears the middle of his term. I hope he will back off from the reimposition of the death penalty, so anti-poor as is his war on druggies.

Back to Charles Manson's California where I may be away for a week and where Manson, et al. killed Sharon Tate, et al., in a most grisly manner in August, 1969. Prez Nixon condemned the accused for "eight murders without reason." A firestorm of protest greeted the startling prejudgment. He apologized and said "the last thing I would do is to prejudice the legal rights of any person, in any circumstances."

Prejudicing the rights of foes is what administration officials have for breakfast in a decaying society.

It may be ironical that the best basketball player in the planet, Lebron James, playing in California, has long gone fishing, while the Warriors and Raptors go for the whole enchilada; he is not even in the playoffs. But, he will come back, as the local Opposition will, to rise above the decay and putrefaction. We are now in Macoy's 1975 when I would get criticized by caring kith and kin for opposing martial law. 1975 was when Uncle Jovy Salonga wrote his Message of Hope which a few of us caring Pinoys signed, pretending not to be afraid. We should maintain our moral stamina.

Who had the motive, opportunity and means to arrange a seven-hour gap on reporting results last May 13-14? Not the Opposition, decidedly. And massive poverty distorts the electoral process. Needs we all have. I have no problem then in granting financial assistance to Chief Justice (CJ) Rene Corona's family for his years in government, as strongly advocated by brilliant retired Supreme Court Justice Art Brion but I have, in his implying that JPE was a railroad man. Impeachment corrected an egregious error, from where I sat, by the people, working through their Congressmen and Senators.

Marbury v. Madison dealt with midnight appointments made by Prez Adams. Aytona v. Castillo, by Prez Garcia. And Sec. 15 of Art. VII of the Constitution does ban appointments during an interdicted period (as I understood it; of course it is said that the SC can correct errors committed below, but, its own, become the law of the land).

Rene's appointment was, in my humble view, not just midnight, but post-midnight, when the new Prez was even then known (May 17, 2010); PNoy did not deserve a monkey wrench to queer the start of his term. Elementary courtesy, which Ambassador Manuel Moran showed in 1953, after it had become clear that Magsaysay had won. Rene should have turned down the appointment, like Moran did, leaving it to the next Prez to name CJ Puno's successor, for a smooth transition. (Doable; I turned down a signed Supreme Court appointment in late January 1987, and life went on. It was just that too many seniors - I was 47 - were in line and to me, public service is its own reward anyway, a line I'd often use and which Rene Corona did in one case).

The impeachment court, led by JPE, certainly with no love lost for the Aquinos whom he would not have done an unmerited favor, corrected GMA's egregious appointment. Rene's earlier midnight appointment in 1998 was not acted on by the Judicial & Bar Council, headed by CJ Andre Narvasa, which believed, correctly, in my humble view, that FVR could no longer appoint, beginning two months before the 1998 elections. CJ Rene's appointment was starkly post-midnight even, from where I sat.

But, again, I support the suggestion of a financial assistance, without any reservation (Rene's father was the wedding Ninong of my Kuya in the mid-60's in Pasig; once I was in their Herran, Paco home). Healing we need in a balkanized society ruled by our own Divider-in-Chief, as it were, for whose good health we all should pray. For the sake of the Motherland.

Decisions made while in royal pain - which we should share – may not be the best.

Saguisag & Associates Lawyers 4045 Bigasan Street, Palanan 1235 Makati Office Nos. (+632) 551-6350/833-4140 Fax No. (+632) 831-2276

oooooo

7
JEWRY, DUE PROCESS 101 AND CJ RENE CORONA

Manila times opinion
<opinion@manilatimes.net>
MTGIF5/31/19

When this piece comes out, I'd most likely be in the U.S., despite my health issues, to be there on June 1. There, and then, my daughter Lara is getting wed. Any father would like to make such a day perfect, to the extent that he would have anything to do with it. This trip is also what her late sainted mother would have wanted to be taken by me, a Super-Takusa (meaning one who loved her, with that kind of passion what whips the blood, and always will).

Our visas were granted only last May 23. We had been booked to fly out the other night. Our visa interview had originally been set on July 2. I had to use my tremendous influence with one who looked like our Foreign Affairs Secretary, to advance the interview. Done. Thank you very many, haha, Pareng Ted and Mareng Louie Locsin. So, off to the wedding, to reconnect with kith and kin, made possible by the DFA's and the Embassy' s kindness, right after my own heart.

It also warmed my heart to see Amazing Grace Poe and Nancy With the Laughing Face Binay, in their proclamation not thrusting their clenched right fist forward, criminal in nations trampled upon by Hitler. The Nazi right fist-bump Aussie Spymaster Nick Warner got hammered, pummelled and pilloried from pillar to post for, after aping Digong naively in the Palace in August 2017.

Another woman with balls, veteran diplomat Delia Albert, had also declined to join the foolish disparagement.

Aging and ailing like me, Digong, six years younger than I, may not have the strength to raise his right hand above the Hitler level. But Dr. Sal Panelo tells us not to worry. Reassuring?

But, really, we should be more sensitive to the sensibilities of the Jewry. 6,000,000 Jews were massacred by Hitler (Digong halved it to 3,000,000 in 2016). We credit Prez Quezon for admitting members of one of the most vilified and persecuted minorities in history. The refugees were fleeing from the Holocaust before World War II.

Our Prez took an oath to do justice to everyone. Instead of convicting anyone by publicity, why not file charges and prove same? Like in the case of the poor Food and Drug Administration chief.

When Nixon blasted Charles Manson for the killing of actress Sharon Tate, criticism was swift and strong; Nixon immediately retreated. Yup, our Prez-elect vows to do justice to everyone. It is not his place to prejudge the guilt or innocence of anyone. For him to adjudge anyone innocent or guilty puts undue pressure on the prosecution, judiciary and witnesses not to embarrass him.

How many have been condemned by Digong, from critics to alleged narco-politicians? He should review our Bill of Rights and the Universal Declaration of Human Rights. We lament the spectacle of judges inhibiting themselves in sensitive widely-publicized cases maybe so as not to risk offending the appointing and promoting power.

We must reintroduce Digong to due process as he nears the middle of his term. I hope he will back off from the reimposition of the death penalty, so anti-poor as is his war on druggies.

Back to Charles Manson's California where I may be away for a week and where Manson, et al.. killed Sharon Tate, et al., in a most grisly manner in August, 1969. Prez Nixon condemned the accused for "eight murders without reason." A firestorm of protest greeted the startling prejudgment. He apologized and said "the last thing I would do is to prejudice the legal rights of any person, in any circumstances."

Prejudicing the rights of foes is what administration officials have for breakfast in a decaying society.

It may be ironical that the best basketball player in the planet, Lebron James, playing in California, has long gone fishing, while the Warriors and Raptors go for the whole enchilada; he is not even in the playoffs. But, he will come back, as the local Opposition will, to rise above the decay and putrefaction. We are now in Macoy's 1975 when I would get criticized by caring kith and kin for opposing martial law. 1975 was when Uncle Jovy Salonga wrote his Message of Hope which a few of us caring Pinoys signed, pretending not to be afraid. We should maintain our moral stamina.

Who had the motive, opportunity and means to arrange a seven-hour gap on reporting results last May 13-14? Not the Opposition, decidedly.. And massive poverty distorts the electoral process. Needs we all have. I have no problem then in granting financial assistance to Chief Justice (CJ) Rene Corona's family for his years in government, as strongly advocated by brilliant retired Supreme Court Justice Art Brion but I have, in his implying that JPE was a railroad man. Impeachment corrected an egregious error, from where I sat, by the people, working through their Congressmen and Senators.

Marbury v. Madison dealt with midnight appointments made by Prez Adams. Aytona v. Castillo, by Prez Garcia. And Sec. 15 of Art. VII of the Constitution does ban appointments during an interdicted period (as I understood it; of course it is said that the SC can correct errors committed below, but, its own, become the law of the land).

Rene's appointment was, in my humble view, not just midnight, but post-midnight, when the new Prez was even then known (May 17, 2010); PNoy did not deserve a monkey wrench to queer the start of his term. Elementary courtesy, which Ambassador Manuel Moran showed in 1953, after it had become clear that Magsaysay had won. Rene should have turned down the appointment, like Moran did, leaving it to the next Prez to name CJ Puno's successor, for a smooth transition. (Doable; I turned down a signed Supreme Court appointment in late January 1987, and life went on. It was just that too many seniors - I was 47 - were in line and to me, public service is its own reward anyway, a line I'd often use and which Rene Corona did in one case).

The impeachment court, led by JPE, certainly with no love lost for the Aquinos whom he would not have done an unmerited favor, corrected GMA's egregious appointment. Rene's earlier midnight appointment in 1998 was not acted on by the Judicial & Bar Council, headed by CJ Andre Narvasa, which believed, correctly, in my humble view, that FVR could no longer appoint, beginning two months before the 1998 elections. CJ Rene's appointment was starkly post-midnight even, from where I sat.

But, again, I support the suggestion of a financial assistance, without any reservation (Rene's father was the wedding Ninong of my Kuya in the mid-60's in Pasig; once I was in their Herran, Paco home). Healing we need in a balkanized society ruled by our own Divider-in-Chief, as it were, for whose good health we all should pray. For the sake of the Motherland.

Decisions made while in royal pain - which we should share - may not be the best.

Saguisag & Associates Lawyers 4045 Bigasan Street, Palanan 1235 Makati Office Nos. (+632) 551-6350/833- 4140 Fax No. (+632) 831-2276

oooooo

8
A PYRRHIC WIN?

Manila times opinion
<opinion@manilatimes.net>
MTGIF5/17/19

Mindanao Development Authority (MinDA) chair Datu Hj Abul Khayr Dangcal Alonto passed on, at 73, last May 9, due to pneumonia, reportedly.

I first heard about him when I returned from abroad in 1971, in San Beda Law, where he, I was told, had dropped out earlier in protest over the Jabidah Massacre. He eventually went underground to fight Marcosian human rights abuses. He never returned to his law studies. He was among the idealistic young patriots whose career path was derailed by martial law. We last met some months ago in the Senate gallery. He did not sound like he had lost the starry notions of our youth.

My gad, my generation is going. I'll be an octogenarian later in the year and doubt that I will follow nonagenarian JPE in age. It's up to the Lord really on how to deal with us mala hierba or masamang damo. As Prez Cory would say, "when the Lord calls, you go." No motion for reconsideration entertained by Sanpiro or Kalawit. And He has just called darling Doris Day, beloved of our generation. And yesterday, I read about Cong. Meniong Teves's passage, at 99. Very old school and we are told he had perfect attendance in the House. giving the people top priority.

Prez Cory ballyhooed me as Saguisag ng Pangulo in my 1987 Senate run (some called me Sagisag na Pang-gulo, which my remarkable pal, Sal Panelo, reminds me of). I landed No. 8 among 24 winners. I didn't have to spend a single singkong duling of my own; in Metro Manila, only Orly Mercado beat me. Harry Roque now says, no half a billion buckaroos? Forget it.

My lawyer-son, Rebo, Jr., won as Makati Councilor, No. 7, despite being deemed unworthy of support by the Iglesia ni Cristo (INC). I had represented parties in conflict with it. I doubt that its captive vote went to JPE, whose firm I assist in the struggle against the powerful group. My respect for INC remains but it should really consider any voter as "a particle of popular sovereignty. " - Jose P. Laurel.

Anyway, ang Saguisag ng Makati (Rebo) had not really consulted me on his run but my kids are old enough to decide for themselves; in case of trouble, I'll be there for them to help decide, etc.. Rebo, with little money, was ready for anything. Last Monday, while waiting for the results, at 10:21:40 pm, he sent this calmative text: "you taught me well. You always get what you pray for. Or something better." Good to hear for a Makateño such as I who attended Makati Elementary School (Bundok) and married Dulce of Barangay Palanan, where I, unable to provide the family a home, was her star boarder for decades.

Elsewhere, our national values continue to deteriorate. Our proud and profane Prez says it is OK to give fare money to voters. Where do we draw the line? In the real world, the fare money could be twenty centavos for tricycles but the voter may be given five hundred bucks, at least, and keep the change. Wink, wink. Part of the culture, says our defeatist Prez.

I didn't have to show my ballot to anyone last Monday. But, the world could see how I was voting anyway given the overcrowded no-privacy small room where we seniors and PWDs (Persons With Disability, or Person Wildly Demented, in my case) were packed. I rightly don't know whether my ballot was accepted or rejected. I just wanted to walk home with my cane as soon as I could. Maybe a distance of 300 meters.

The INC's, Bro. Mike's, Brother Eddie's or Pastor Quiboloy' s endorsement, if any, may not make one win but lack of it can make him lose. I prefer my Catholic Church's injunction: follow your conscience, not that of some high priest.

"Point to me someone who doesn't buy votes," Digong dares the polity. Well, my son didn't nor did I in 1987. I am sure countless others didn't, either. Rhetoric has a powerful effect on human conduct. Digong's needless observations or malapropisms will continue to haunt our anti-poor electoral process. The coming elections will enhance dominant pro-wealthy dynasts, as our values, institutions and processes continue to slide down and deteriorate. The anti-poor death penalty may be back. The anti-poor drug war may intensify. And the Chinese will claim what is ours and continue to come and do tasks Pinoys can do, treating us as its 24th province.

The presidency must be on a commanding moral high ground given man's frailties. The Prez should not go down the low road.

I didn't vote for JPE but would not have minded if he had won. I did vote for Serge Osmeña. Experienced voices, not echoes. The Senate shouldn't be a House clone.

My heart goes out to fearless Jojo Binay, with whom I shared foxholes during martial law, and the Estradas, with whom I fought for the Constitution, and whose pain I also share.

Democracy may have been the biggest loser last Monday, even if every proclaimed winner deserves the benefit of the doubt. I hope and pray that no Senator will treat his/her post as a sideline, hobby or diversion. Or whose only foolish question if asked by Digong to jump from a high-rise would be - "from what floor, Sir?"

Else, we may lament with Pyrrhus of Epirus, another victory such as this over the Romans, and we are undone (in one only too real sense).

Apre Digong, le deluge?

His current dominative position may be likened to Macoy's standing in 1975, three years after he inflicted martial law upon a nation of busabos at alipin of the Kastilaloys, the Brits, the Kanos, the Hapones, the Kanos again, the Ilokanos and now, the Davaoeños.

Today, the reopened deep wounds are arguably self-inflicted by and large by our very own timorous people.

Power does not corrupt. It only tends to, per Lord Acton who then apodictically said, "absolute power corrupts absolutely." That is what last Monday may mean yet. I hope and pray not and would like to see a transformed, not transmogrified, leader ushering us into his personal 1976, when Macoy finally listened to international criticism and started military trials. We don't need any old black magic that seems to have the nation under its spell.

In April 6, 1978 Metro Manila erupted in a noise barrage but Macoy and Imelda shut out LABAN, 21-0, including Ninoy. who eventually put himself where his mouth was: The Filipino is worth dying for.

Saguisag & Associates Lawyers 4045 Bigasan Street, Palanan 1235 Makati Office Nos. (+632) 551-6350/833- 4140 Fax No. (+632) 831-2276

oooooo

9
MY SENATE LIST; ON FOREIGN GRANTS AND FUNDS

May 9, 2019 <ravslaw@gmail.com> wrote:

To my list of 14 Senate candidates I respectfully and humbly recommend to vote for, may I add Nancy Binay among those to be considered to be picked on Monday. 14 din, gaya po ng listahan ni Brother Mike Velarde. I am firm though on MATH GRAD, Macalintal, Aquino, Tañada, Hilbay, Gutoc, Roxas, Alejano and Diokno, sure to "fiscalize", a quaint Filipinism. For the last four seats, COPPAB, Colmenares, Osmeña, Poe, Pimentel, Alunan, Binay. Like Brother Mike, I do have more than a baker's dozen. My final four would depend on how I may see him or her as for a truly independent Senate, not for anyone who will simply ask Digong, "from what floor, Sir," if asked to jump to a conclusion from some high-rise. Voices, not Echoes, we need in a vibrant democracy.

I also would like to see a sense of work ethic, approximating Manong Ernie Maceda and me. We were never late, much less absent, in our time. The people should have first claim on a Senator's time, energy and attention in the chamber, a small deliberative body, whose 24 members should toil, not for self, but country. We cannot underrate anyone's capacity for work, change and growth. Comparisons may be odious but let us look at our 1987-92 Senate; there, I initially had an inferiority complex, recalling that Diokno, Estrada-Kalaw, Laurel, Pelaez, Marcos, Manglapus, Mitra, Puyat, Recto, Rodrigo, Salonga, Sumulong, Tañada, Tolentino, Ziga, et al. cross-fertilized ideas in coruscating edifying debates.

In my time though, Salonga (Harvard, Yale), presided. Others attended Central Universidad de Madrid (one), Cornell (one), Harvard (seven), Michigan (one) and Wellesley and Sorbonne (one). We got our degrees through toil and hard work. Much beloved Amang Rodriguez did not have such credentials but is credited for being a hardworking focused Senate Prez for a decade, in the service of our people. Ka Blas Ople didn't have much formal schooling but excelled and shone through reading and writing. Who will be the new Amangs and Ka Blases?

I wouldn't like to sound elitist and the 2019 Senate after next week can also demonstrate a splendid work ethic, as everyone in the 1987-92 Senate did. All of us took well-studied differing positions, on the military bases issue, for instance.

Accepting foreign funding and help, without more, I won't take against anyone, if used to better oneself to serve the cause of truth and our people. For the record, I have been a beneficiary of the Ford Foundation (full scholarship in Harvard Law), Fulbright (travel grant, privileged to be labelled a Fulbright Pioneer by the U.S. Embassy), Asia Foundation (travel grant), maybe the National Endowment for Democracy (trip to Indonesia early this millennium but I was also there pre-Edsa'86, courtesy of another donor). I have also forgotten the donor and am not certain as to pre-Edsa'86 Indonesia, but if my fading memory is true, I there detected a strong nationalist anti-China sentiment even then). I got help from a foreign religious group I saved from being prosecuted and expelled from here in 1997-98, thanks to Acting Justice Secretary Bebot Bello, a fellow activist, who understood religious freedom as a basic human and constitutional right.

Named in 1982 as Human Rights Grantee of the State Department in its International Visitors Program, MABINI voted 13-2 for me to accept the grant; I was outvoted, with only Joey Lina voting NO with me; our non-voting Honorary Chair, Tanny Tañada, also objected, but MABINI observed the majoritarian principle).

A Catholic Foundation sponsored me a for a year (1968-69) in Berkeley on a non-degree program, enabling me to read cover-to-cover the Jerusalem Bible, all the eleven volumes of the Durants' Story of Civilization, the Anatomy of a Revolution by Crane Brinton, etc.. Religion team teachers John T. Noonan, Jr. and David Daube guided, but never leaned on, me, aside from giving me "that rarest commodity in American academic life: leisure . . . the chance to read and reflect without the pressure of any immediate commitment to being, or pretending to be, useful," per Lon L. Fuller, my Harvard Jurisprudence teacher.

Anyway, no one could have convinced me not to vote No! on the bases in September. 1991. Not one donor tried to strong-arm me on my views. They just let me alone, by and large. Our conversations were always amiable and constructive, even if contrasting.

Who among the senatorial candidates would ape Manong Ernie and me, never late, much less absent? Yes, the people had first crack on our limited time, energy and attention. Hard diligent government workers. Other qualifications are secondary. But, we do have to arrest the decay and deterioration of our values, institutions and processes which would be exacerbated with an obsequious Senate. An Echo Chamber we don't need.

Among the good Senators now is certainly Ping Lacson. But, if he pooh-poohs the latest ongoing distribution of $1,500 each to a qualified human rights victim and thinks the aging, ailing rights beneficiaries deserve more, which they certainly do, he should craft a law to supplement what R.A. No. 10368 gave. This month certain victims are getting another $1,500.00 from class suit specialist Bob Swift, on top of two prior distributions. The beneficiaries, by and large, spent no money or effort to collect. The effort was wholly financed by Bob's firm, which just told them there is money to spend for sustenance, including medicines.

A Pennsylvania article entitled SWIFT JUSTICE recounts that three decades later, Bob's first-ever human rights class action lawsuit remains the poignant gold standard. Bob remembers one deposition that needed to be postponed after the court reporter broke down while transcribing a witness account of the salvaging of her four children.

By the early '80's, he was following our anti-Macoy movement. punctuated by Ninoy's 1983 salvaging. In 1986, the Marcoses fled to Hawaii. "That gave me the idea to put together a case to obtain compensation for all the victims, from a guy who was supposedly one of the richest people in the world, a multibillionaire, who had now come to the U.S.," he recalled.

So he came and conferred with the likes of JoeMari Velez. One problem: never before had a former president of a foreign country been brought to trial in the U.S.. To establish jurisdiction, Bob unearthed the Alien Tort Statute, passed by the U.S.'s first Congress in 1789. It gave aliens the right to sue in U.S. courts for violations of international human rights. How? "The concept was to have a single trial using the concept of command responsibility - that he's responsible for the abuses at the hands of his troops," Bob said. Fair warning to the world.

Bob remembers the handwritten sign an old woman raised as she sat outside a remote rural barangay. It read "Thank you, Mr. Swift."

I join her. Bob follows the Quaker faith, for whom finding justice for victims became an all-consuming quest for him, fierce resistance from our and the American governments, notwithstanding.

Bob deserves gratitude - the most beautiful flower in the garden of the heart - and support, I submit, not baseless criticism. He is doing what we should be doing. Stay as sweet as you are, Bob. And the Prez should not stay as insensitive and uncaring about human rights as he nears June 30, time for a mid-course correction, beginning with his profanity. Good people change others, better ones change the system, the best change, themselves. I am not for his ouster but for his transformation, not transmogrification.

And thank you, too, and goodbye, Karina Constantino-David. Even before Ninoy was salvaged, you and Becky Demetillo, fearless patriots, comprised a splendid presence with your inspirational duets as Inang Laya in anti-fascist gatherings.

Saguisag & Associates Lawyers 4045 Bigasan Street, Palanan 1235 Makati Office Nos. (+632) 551-6350/833-4140 Fax No. (+632) 831-2276

oooooo

10
INDONESIA SHOWS WAY TO GO; TIMEO SERES. . . .

MTGIF5/3/19
Manila times opinion
<opinion@manilatimes.net>

Two Aprils ago, it was reported that Indonesia blew up and sank another 81 fishing boats for poaching. 'Twas April 1, but no April Fool's Day.

One April 1 account on astig Indonesia's sangfroid follows:

"Indonesia on Saturday (April 1) blew up and sank 81 more fishing boats caught poaching in its waters. This takes the total number of boats confiscated and destroyed to 317 since October 2014 when President Joko Widodo took office and called for tougher action against poachers. Among those sunk so far are fishing boats from [various countries, including ours], as well as one from China. Maritime Affairs and Fisheries Minister Susi Pudjiastuti, . . . called it a victory for Indonesia' s war against illegal fishing." She delights in being called "nasty" and says many other vessels carrying Indonesian flags "were really under Beijing' s control," which factor didn't intimidate her at all.

President Joko had said that Indonesia suffered annual substantial losses from poaching in its vast territorial waters. After he was elected, he put Susi in the Fisheries Ministry and she has been the "nasty" point-woman behind his plan to revive the country' s fisheries industries. (How many of us dummy for aliens?)

"Experts have said the increased security in Indonesia's waters against illegal fishing, . . . comes amid tensions in the region fuelled by Beijing' s overlapping claims in the South China Sea. China claims almost all of the sea lane, while Vietnam, the Philippines, Malaysia, Brunei and Taiwan have overlapping claims. Jakarta is not a party to the disputes but became concerned after Beijing declared in March [2016] that the waters around the Natunas, which lie within Indonesia' s exclusive economic zone, are part of its `traditional fishing grounds'.

"In what appeared to many as a veiled response to Beijing' s claim, Mr. Joko in June last year, boarded a warship for a visit to the waters off the Natuna Islands."

Something like this visit was what some of us remember was the plighted word of Digong, to jetski to the disputed West

Philippine Sea area, a vital gesture. But here, he is no Joko, just a joker, NATO, No Action Talk Only.

Our Prez has just returned from China, skipping another gala dinner - also a no-show the , other day - reminding the naughty that he may well be, to some critics, our National Migraine. (Mine is in trying to tell his 40% front-page stuff from the 60% comic relief. War with Canada, our friend, over trash? May we not just bury it here - surely we have the technology - and simply demand damages, and prosecute, where warranted?) His people gush over the deals and gifts he brought home from China. I wish.

For my part, I am reminded of "timeo danaos et dona ferentes," of Virgil, in Aenid, part of my Major in English course. I fear the Greeks even when they come bearing gifts. Do we now have many creeping and soon to be galloping Trojan Horses?

Timeo seres et dona ferentes. By my lonesome maybe(?), I fear the Chinese even when they come bearing gifts, displacing our workers, driving up the cost of real estate, luring us to a possible debt trap, mocking Digong's drug war with their shabu shipments, and appropriating what is ours and denying our fishermen a livelihood. Hating-Kapatid is Digong's curious formula of what is arguably fully ours.

It seems we are now told to follow Confucius' counsel, if rape is inevitable, just lie back and enjoy it.

After nearly three years we now have worse traffic, water and power shortages, drought, tremors, shabu worth billions, and worsening massive poverty, for which Digong may not be entirely to blame but mishandling the sea dispute is another matter altogether. Let's pray he finds the correct way.

But, while most any other Prez may lead the nation in praying to our God, Digong however insults, dismisses, downgrades or minimizes Him. Discombobulating. Not the way to go, from where I sit.

The U.S. and China may both be devils but as Ninoy Aquino would say, better the devil we know rather than one we don't. In foreign relations, given the crucial role of the Senate in same, all the more we should think of my MATH GRAD COPPA formula, Macalintal, Aquino, Tañada, Hilbay, Gutoc, Roxas, Alejano, Diokno, Colmenares, Osmeña, Pope, Pimentel and Alunan (there will have to be some Unlucky Thirteenth). If enough of them win, democracy is saved, or strengthened. Cheers!

In Masses, I am mildly surprised at the cheers I hear, as if it were the SONA, twice recently in the middle of the ceremony. I am hardly getting used - at the end of Mass, to the applause - now increasing. Later, a Mass may sound like the State of the Nation Address, where every time a Prez inhales, the sipsips dutifully applaud.

Even sorta novel was the sight in church of one woman in short shorts, which could really compete for attention. I have no recollection if she was young or old. How could one tell when focused on the distracting legs? Even in ballroom dancing, some women display a lot of gam. Needlessly. (Rick Ramos and I dancexercised the other night; he had reminded me of Indonesian amazon Susi.)

Another distraction. Traffic, dictating the tempo of our lives, complicates our skeds, compounded by our mania for pix-taking. Kodakan.. We don't seem to hurry, nor to worry, but find the time in our short visit here on earth to stop and smell the flowers. - Walter Hagen. Nice? But, nastiness is at times required in the national interests.

The Indonesians have a nasty Fisheries chief, a woman who would not hesitate to blow up foreign vessels staying into her country' s waters. Not even China is spared, and it did not retaliate.

Taiwan, Vietnam, Malaysia and Indonesia the Chinese don't kick around cuz they have shown PUSO. Fisheries issues comprised one problem in the Second War between the U.S. and Britain in the 1800s. When I was little, I loved the Kanos and hated the Japanese but at 14, I was charmed by pert sprinter Atsuko Nambu in the 2nd Asian Games here in 1954. Japan is a very good friend today, an ally against China's Irridentism.

Timeo seres. . . . I, along with many Pinoys, now fear the Chinese, who need to do more that we may be allies again, as we were in WWII against Japan. So, no permanent friends or enemies, only permanent interests. - Lord Palmerston. So, anytime we deal and shake hands with the U.S., China, whichever, to count our fingers afterwards.

Meantime, I bid goodbye and thank Art Bernales, my fellow Bedan and my former Senate staffer. Gone at 50. Cardiac. The Lord's will. In the 80's we met and together chased rainbows for those whose cares and causes have been our concern, and the dream shall never die, to borrow from Ted Kennedy and Chopin.

Saguisag & Associates Lawyers 4045 Bigasan Street, Palanan 1235 Makati Office Nos. (+632) 551-6350/833-4140 Fax No. (+632) 831-2276

oooooo

11
CALAMITOUS IRRIDENTISM AND LEBENSRAUM

MTGIF4/26/19
Manila times opinion
<opinion@manilatimes.net>

For full disclosure, if my memory is true, my 1967-68 Harvard Law full scholarship was funded by the Ford Foundation.

My first memory of Kanos were of GIs ten feet tall, giving me more choclits than I could use, singing "You are my sunshine, . . ." The Times introduced me to the New York Yankees in my Makati Elementary school days with the riveting columns of Red Smith (and in caging, the elegant NCAA reports of Tony Siddayao). Still, I want the Kanos and the Chinese to leave us alone. Meeting China halfway - Digong's reported formula - sounds exorbitant, even extortionate, appeasement of China's Hitler. Xi's Irridentism reminds me of Hitler's Lebensraum.

Assume that PNoy left a mess by going to arbitration. But, surely the legal way cannot be wrong. Isn't it up to his successor to clean up the mess, if that? Instead, we appease the regional super-bully which doesn't honor agreements (the 2012 mutual agreement to withdraw from the disputed area). Talaga pong mga makong at magulang yata.

I know Sheila Coronel, Malou Mangahas and Ellen Tordesillas, having been in the trenches with them during the dark years. Maria Ressa I may know only from afar. They are pros in this age where ownership matters less as we watch CNN, BBC, etc. all the time. More speech, not less. To silence dissent would be calamitous.

Last Monday, calamity; where we worked in Palanan, Makati, started shaking violently. Then a brownout. Metro Manila might not have been really badly damaged but elsewhere, far worse. Then, the next day, Eastern Visayas. It is another unifying fear, of the Big One. (BTW, "[a]n earthquake shoved the 1989 World Series to the periphery of the nation's attention," George F. Will wrote in Men at Work - The Craft of Baseball, a gift that another true pro, Pocholo Romualdez kindly gave me.)

The fear of China has provided a unifying grievance for the people which the Palace may not ignore. Thus the new macho stance assumed by Digong. But, after the elections, what? Return to *wala-naman-po-tayong-magagawa* pusillanimosity? The Viets and Malaysia, *may magagawa po?* They have guts, moxie or gumption. Back to Chamberlain's appeasement in the face of an Asian Hitler?

Now, the seemingly aggressive stance on Sabah, to open another> front, with Malaysia. In the 60's, while in law school and years after, I was for pressing our claim to it, as bannered by Prez Macapagal.

In 1980, I flew to Kota Kinabalu. Mouth-watering virgin forests, lotsa oil, etc.. But, by then, Macoy had become passive;

no successor has revived the claim of dominion, until now, when DFA Secretary Ted Locsin resurrected the issue. I applaud his initiative to pull the matter out of the back burner for a definitive resolution.

But, should what the Sabahans want matter? Were I a Sabahan, and made to determine and choose between Kuala Lumpur and Manila, which would I pick? I think we should quietly survey how the Sabahans really feel about us in Imperial Manila or Imperial Davao. Do they long, yearn and pine to be governed by us? In short, I now feel that we may not ignore the Sabahans's preference. Else, it may cost us more than the Mamasapano 44; are we ready to "pay any price, bear any burden, meet any hardship, oppose any foe, etc." - JFK? Yup, what are we to do? Digong has to tell us.

What I would also like to know is what government has done to get millions of dollars on the latest success of lawyers Bob Swift, Rod Domingo and Ruben Fruto. Without them, where would the victims and government be? Sila po yata ang nagsaing, pamahalaan po ang kakain? What has government done to get $4M? It should tell us.

Absent Bob, how much would the victims and government have received by now from litigation? He has had two previous distributions. Soon, the third, for the aging, ailing cash-strapped gross human rights violations victims. A better deal that government dreams of may just be brought to our doorsteps, just to lie there and die there, to borrow from the poignant Mona Lisa lyrics.

So, we need human rights Voices in the Senate. We don't need mere Echoes there, the reason why Koko Pimentel, son of Nene, jailed by Macoy four times, should be returned, along with Bam Aquino, son of a fellow Bedan, and Grace Poe, the daughter of a fellow Bedan.

Be ready with codigos, we are advised. Mine, MATH GRAD COPPA for Macalintal Aquino Tañada Hilbay Gutoc Roxas Alejano Diokno Colmenares (another Bedan) Osmeña Pimentel Poe Alunan. Too bad one has to be dropped from my codigo of a Baker's Dozen.

Mar Roxas and PNoy continue to be lambasted for Mamasapano. I think they should answer only to their conscience and history. Mamasapano, to me, was not a failure but a 75% success. Notorious terrorist Marwan was bagged on whose head was at least $5M. I only see it as a failure in that no justice, attention or assistance has been given to slain Sara, 5, and her parents, who were wounded when their home was strafed. By whom? - should be probed. Silence. Sapagka't sila po ba ay mga Muslim lamang? Like the 20,000 Muslims, et al. killed on February 7-8, 1974 in Jolo by our military? Or the 1,500 slain in September, 1974 in a Palimbang mosque, with the women raped, again by our military?

44 heroes killed? Sad, let's honor them as truly deserving heroes, but members of Special Forces know the risk. Soldiers get killed regularly elsewhere, with only their loved ones noticing and caring.

No Prez is transformed to perfection by being so elected. They remain as fallible as you and I and should not be punished legally for alleged errors of judgment made in good faith. Else, no Prez is safe for remaining mortal. Yes, he answers only to his conscience and to history.

Did I err and land on the wrong side of history for scrapping the Bataan nuke plant? I was a key player on it, following Chernobyl in 1986, as Cabinet and Senate Committee Chair on the matter. The two bodies unanimously endorsed my position. Were I in error, FVR, Erap, GMA and PNoy could have corrected fallible me. I don't recall Manong Johnny, an able lawyer, opposing my recommendation in the Cabinet and the Senate. Defense Secretary Delfin Lorenzana, not a lawyer, ably disagrees with JPE, citing the Constitution and international pacts.

Indeed, the only perfect official I know is another Bedan, Supreme Court Justice Gregorio Perfecto.

Seriously, a perfect storm may hit us next month if the Otso Diretso Voices do not do well and only the Echoes get elected.

Is the U.S. afraid of China as Digong taunts? It might well be, but it fights. But, even more so, are we, or should we be, afraid? Last Tuesday, we bannered "Duterte to China: Let's meet halfway" - Should it not be 100% of what is ours and let the bargaining begin? But, to give up half right off seems to ensure that we'll end up at the shorter end of the stick of what is 100% ours. Di po yata namimili si Digong sa Divisoria from the Chinese vendors who cannot even speak Tagalog or English. There my late wife and her siblings validated that when the going gets tough, the tough go shopping, nickeling-and-diming the tinderas.

All the more do we need the Otso Diretso and like-minded candidates to ask the foolish questions of the day. Not only, "from what floor, Sir?" - if told by Digong to jump out of a high-rise window.

The disasters we are having will be nothing compared to what may happen on May 13, when Digong may become super-executive, super-legislature, super-judiciary and a one-man-continuing-constitutional-convention as the ramparts of democracy fall without a struggle. Wotta calamity it would be.

He's having blood tests every other day? Hmmmm. Would suchfequency affect moods and judgments? We have to ask real doctors.

Saguisag & Associates Lawyers 4045 Bigasan Street, Palanan 1235 Makati Office Nos. (+632) 551-6350/833-4140 Fax No. (+632) 831-2276

Oooooo

12
VOTE FOR VOICES, NOT ECHOES, IN A SCOFFLAW NATION

Apr 17, 2019 <ravslaw@gmail.com>

The last time (also the first) I saw Paris, Notre Dame was a must-see. There, my Dulce and I went - in December 1970 on our way home - to the iconic many-splendored cathedral, attended Mass, and heard songs sung in French. Heavenly. Back to earth and mundane matters.

May Digong correct "in due time" his statement of assets and liabilities (SAL) and statement of assets, liabilities, net worth, etc. (SALNs), as if he had a choice? The deadlines are in R.A. No. 3019 and R.A. No. 6713. The first is tough; the latter has a review and compliance procedure under its Sec. 10. One must be given a chance to correct any lapse, on his own, or after his attention is called by some review and compliance officer.

Under the 1973 and 1987 Constitutions, on top of Digong's annual salary (nearly P5,000,000,000.00), he is barred from receiving any emolument "from any other source." The 1935 Constitution, only from any other government source. Is getting from other sources on top of his monthly pay of just under P400,000.00 the reason for possible correction, completion or, heaven forbid, embroidery?

As co-author and floor sponsor of what became R.A. No. 6713, on ethical norms, I didn't intend to be strict with anyone except in case of recalcitrance. An initial noncompliance may be corrected but bullheadedness may be punished. I can recall instances when a case was dismissed in the Sandiganbayan absent such chance to correct.

We also made it easy and convenient for one to get a copy of SALN on payment of photocopying, mailing and certification costs (Sec. 8[C]3) but the Bigger House and the Supreme Court have made the process a via dolorosa. What are they hiding? Fear of being kidnapped? Felons have a way of knowing who are kidnap-worthy. If the would-be victims remain terrorized, then they should just leave government service and plant camote. One must learn to live dangerously at a time of gridlocked traffic, water, power and parking shortages, conducive to road rage, and a lot of needless presidential cussing amid a threat to suspend the privilege of habeas corpus in a barbaric regime with massive poverty and no respect for due process and for human life and dignity.

Yet, a popular Prez? Go figure.

Over the years I have asked my students to show proof of compliance by anyone in government with Sec. 7 of the Tolentino SAL law of 1960. Only one managed to comply, with an old one filed before the Salonga-Saguisag SALN law of 1989. I now promise them a final grade of 80% if they can show that anyone in government has complied with Sec. 7 of R.A. No. 3019 which requires "a true, detailed and sworn statement of assets and liabilities, including a statement of the amounts and sources of income, the amount of his personal and family expenses and the amount of income taxes paid for the last preceding calendar year." This requirement, the SolGen correctly cited on pages 28-29 of his petition for quo warranto against Chief Justice Meilou Sereno. Yet, neither he nor Digong has so complied therewith in the copies I have. Haz lo que digo, no lo que hago. Do as I say, not as I do. No fair.

The Commission on Civil Service consolidated Sec. 7 of R.A. No. 3019 with Sec. 8 of R.A. No. 6713 in one form but retreated when the Bigger House howled. Millions of scofflaws. Why not have an amnesty then with a clause that future violations thereafter would be dealt with more severely?

Weird that my R.A. No. 6713 was used to render jobless legitimate appointee Meilou Sereno and illegitimate post-midnight appointee Rene Corona, with all due respect. Rene was named Chief Justice on May 17, 2010, after Noynoy had clearly won, when GMA was a mere caretaker, for a smooth transition, not an undertaker.

The SolGen, who had nothing to do with the latest recovery from the Marcoses' ill-gotten wealth, would like to stop the payment of $1,500.00 each to thousands of human rights victims next month, the third such distribution by Bob & Co.. Government, which did and spent nothing, will also get $4M, through the efforts of Bob Swift and Rod Domingo and Ruben Fruto, who took over from the late JoeMari Velez.

A falsity I saw in another paper last Saturday said that "elitist" Cory blocked that human rights class suit. "In 1986-1987, the elite through the then-president opposed the filing of such a suit. She mobilized the government to stop, question, and thwart the suit. . . . [the] president and the first post-Marcos Congress wanted to deny Marcos human rights victims compensation and indemnification, . . ." Huh?

I was in the Palace and sssh, the first post-Marcos Congress. and heard of no such Cory opposition to Bob's suit whose firm took care of my expenses when I went to Hawaii in 1992. I heard the jury award $1.2B as one form of damages. I also aided in the case of the Archimedes Trajano heirs against Imee Marcos. The $4.5M+-award remains unpaid.

What motivation, pray tell, would Cory have to thwart the suit? Joker Arroyo, Nene Pimentel, Tito Guingona, Bobbit Sanchez, Jun Factoran, Jojo Binay, Dodo Sarmiento, Ed Araullo, Hessie Mallilin, and others, like myself, were in government. We would probably have resigned in protest. Her family was the victim of the most well-known human rights violation, the "salvaging" of Ninoy. A game-changer. The aforesaid modern fairy tale must be thwarted. It was the military grousing against us, alleged Commies in government; no compensation bill (I filed S.B. No. 1932) could have gone far in the coup-plagued administration.

Senate Prez Jovy Salonga, Bob, Rod, Ruben and I would consult. And I, as Cory, Jr., was authorized to tell the military to cooperate in Bob's efforts to gain access to intelligence files, helping the case move along. Had Cory blocked the suit, one could imagine the uproar. My Senate staff, such as Cy del Callar, liaised with the Palace and the PCGG (Presidential Commission on Good Government).

In a class suit, a plaintiff spends nothing. Melvin Belli filed suit for 21 named plaintiffs; the American Civil Liberties Union, assisted by the late Romy Capulong, filed suit for only three (JoMa Sison, Ramon Sison and Jaime Piopongco). The last two were not class suits and were ordered consolidated with Bob's.

Our age-old problem remains, a circular firing squad we are.. Fine, if we will all face outward and shoot the enemy, not one another.

We could accomplish so much more if no one cares who gets the credit, or falsifies recent history. On the blame game, I am not certain Irene Marcos should be grouped by Ateneo with Ferdie, Macoy, Imee and Bongbong. Too young at the time? She merits the benefit of the doubt. And I hail Ateneo for the Blue Babble Batallion memorably demoing against extrajudicial killings at one UAAP halftime.

I agree with Ka Pepe Diokno; we are all bundles of biases and prejudices. As William James said, we think we think when we in fact merely rearrange our prejudices. I respect anyone's right to be prejudiced and would not compel him to like what I like and dislike what I dislike. The right to speak includes the right not to speak. The right to write includes the right not to. The heart has its reasons of which reason knows nothing, per Pascal. Freedom of conscience.

Think then not of the next elections alone, but of future generations. I endorse Otso Diretso, to be joined by Serge Osmeña, who fought Macoy, and Raffy Alunan, a disciple of Uncle Jovy Salonga along with Pilo Hilbay, in Bantay Katarungan. We need Voices, not Echoes. The human rights community supplies the former, namely, Chel Diokno and Erin Tanada. Fruits does not fall or roll far from the tree. Gary Alejano is a welcome figure from the military. Romy Macalintal, for his advocacy of the rights of seniors like me and his election expertise. Samira Gutoc, a principled Muslim woman, would be a clear plus. Of course, Mar Roxas and Bam Aquino, I support on their own, and in grateful memory of Gerry Roxas and of fellow Benedictines Ninoy and Cory, with their Designer Genes. Ten. I have room for one more, after Grace Poe, the daughter of another fellow Bedan, FPJ, whose middle name was Decency. Eleven. Militant Neri Colmenares also, another fellow Bedan, for the 12th slot.

In May then, Otso Diretso, plus four, not those who, when told by Digong to jump from a high-rise, would probably ask, "from what floor, Sir?" - and jump to their conclusion.

Democracy requires a credible Opposition. Vibrant voices, not effete echoes.

Saguisag & Associates Lawyers 4045 Bigasan Street, Palanan 1235 Makati Office Nos. (+632) 551-6350/833-4140 Fax No. (+632) 831-2276

Oooooo

13
HONESTY AND MODEST LIVES IN THE CONSTITUTION

MTGIF3/30/19
Manila times opinion
<opinion@manilatimes.net>

Sec. 27 of Art. II of the Constitution, on State Policies, says: "The State shall maintain honesty and integrity in the public service. . . ." Honesty is not required in public office? Is it a dead letter in this administration?

And what about the integrity of our territory? Not for Neville Chamberlain's policy of appeasement, I, recalling Mactan, Balangiga, Bataan and Bessang Pass, let alone Cuba,

Vietnam and Somalia, readily signed the Statement of Support for Secretary Albert del Rosario and Ombudswoman Conchita Carpio Morales, which said:

"We laud the brave act [issuing the Communication] taken by former Foreign Affairs Secretary Albert del Rosario and former Ombudswoman Conchita Carpio Morales in filing a case against Chinese President Xi Jinping before the International Court (ICC) for the `atrocious actions of Chinese officials in the South China Sea and within Philippine territory.

"It is about time that concerned Filipinos take [took?] a stand against the Chinese government for its aggressive actions in the South China Sea including territory which belongs to the Philippine government. We stand fully behind [the duo] in whatever other steps that need to be taken to bring this case forward and call on all Filipino citizens, concerned about loss of control over sovereign Philippine territory; loss of livelihood for thousands of our fisherfolk; food security; massive destruction of our marine environment; and loss of control over a strategic waterway, to stand up and be counted before it is too late."

As Al Smith would say, "let's look at the record." The historic Communication is a deposition for history, that not everyone slept. Not for me is becoming America's 51st state.

Senators Tanny Tañada, Pepe Diokno, Soc Rodrigo, Jovy Salonga, Ninoy Aquino, et al., openly resisted martial law, as such depositions for history, the odds notwithstanding. They have landed on the right side of history, like Fidel Castro's Cuba si! Yanqui no!, confident that history would absolve him. La historia me absolvera! - Fidel boomed in 1953.

Becoming China's 24th province also leaves me cold, for that matter. If the latter, going to Hong Kong wouldn't be foreign travel anymore. Otherwise, Digong is correct in banning unnecessary foreign trips of bureaucrats. But, should it not apply to himself, first and foremost?

Sec. 1 of Art. XI of the Constitution on Accountability of Public Officers says that "[p]ublic office is a public trust. Public officers and employees must at all times be accountable to the people, serve them with utmost . . . integrity, . . . act with patriotism, and lead modest lives."

Only last month, to mark the birth anniversary of his fave partner, no place in the Philippines would do (but would, presumably, for his other partners). Hong Kong it had to be. Can one imagine any other high official, or even a low one, doing it? In our face. Maybe even with the expressive middle finger "You are No. 1" gesture.

Natcherly, security, media people and staff would have to accompany a Prez anywhere. How much did that trip cost us? His being uneasy in Manila, means a lot of travel expense of frequent Davao-Manila-Davao trips. Marrying Honeylet and living in Malacañang would save on expenses and set the proper example to the young, particularly to those celebrities even bragging being preggy without the benefit of matrimony.

The Philippine Star had a February 17, 2019 account on Digong's unannounced Hong Kong trip to celebrate Honeylet's birthday with his family [how many families does our Tsikboy Prez have anyway?] that weekend.

"The 73-year-old president and his security aides were seen in a shop of casual wear designer and retailer Uniqlo at the World Trade Centre in Causeway Bay last Saturday, . . .

"The report said some shoppers recognized the president but no one greeted him. [No selfies? No lips-to-lips osculation, either.]

"Duterte's former aide Christopher Go said the president's daughter Kitty was the one who requested for [sic] the trip as a `gift.' [What does the Commission on Audit say?]

"`They have done this before when President Duterte was still mayor of Davao City. The weekend getaway is for rest and recreation," Go said in a statement. [Why is he still issuing statements?]

Haz lo que digo, no lo que hago. Do as I say, not do as I do, Digong tells the rest of our countrymen in government, in a scofflaw country of decaying values.

The Commission on Civil Service lauds spenthrift Digong's travel-ban directive, without saying *"di po imperialismo, di po komunismo, kundi kayo po mismo, ang problema,"*

Presidential extravagance I can see in Digong whining that the presidential salary (now just under P400,000.00 monthly) isn't enough to support his two families.

I also see extravagance and myopia in the Senate's desire to have a new building in the Global City. It will perpetuate the aberration of having a bicameral legislature housed far apart, which conduces to waste, inefficiency and acrimony. Putting them in one building or compound would result in economy, efficiency and amity. Is it another *Onli in d Pilipins* anomaly? The national penitentiary should be moved out of Muntinlupa. The two Houses can then move there, for certain members to serve terms in office and another term in jail. The Bataan nuke plant is another candidate for pork-squabbling lawmakers, and an exasperated public can pray for a meltdown.

Seriously, back to honesty, to paraphrase Judge Learned Hand, that virtue, along with liberty, lies in the hearts of men and women; when it dies there, no constitution, no law, no court can save it. Like Chamberlain giving away Czechoslovakia, we are giving up part of our territory, to appease the arguably Irridentist dragon.

Happy 74th birth anniversary anyway, Mr. President, yesterday. *Pilipins na lang po tayo*, I see, and appreciate. Not celebrating it but just sleep the day away? On this, we're on the same page. Left to my own devices, I would not mark my birth anniversaries either but my late wife and kids won't leave me alone.

Anyway, I see where Digong, showing class the Ayalas have demonstrated on water shortage, admits that the bloody, messy war on drugs has not succeeded, as indeed it has failed all over the world. It has been anti-poor, like the death penalty he wants returned by public hanging. We should follow the UN General Assembly developments on the drug problem, stressing the need for a humane and compassionate policy reflecting a deep concern for human rights. And am I glad and proud that the Catholic Church opposes the anti-poor death penalty.

I remain staunchly opposed to extrajudicial killing and judicial murder.

Saguisag & Associates Lawyers 4045 Bigasan Street, Palanan 1235 Makati Office Nos. (+632) 551-6350/833-4140 Fax No. (+632) 831-2276

oooooo

14
NATIONAL MIGRAINE?

MTGIF3/23/19
Manila times opinion
opinion@manilatimes.net

Our *makwento* President continues to be too talkative for comfort, from where I sit. Better left unsaid for instance: "I don't care if priests die," prattled he. Petty. Divisive. Needless negativity offensive to practicing, if trying-hard, Catholics.

I see no benefit from what may arguably be pasable for a parochial city Meyor. But, a very busy Pangulo is nobler, and expected to stick to the high ground, beginning in language, as a role model of the youth we try hard to teach to be empathetic, kind, courteous and considerate. Repetitive vilification does not become a Prez, who is Prez of all our people, and Digong vowed, on June 30, 2016, to do justice to everyone.

John Donne may be said to differ with our quarrelsome Prez, saying no man is an island entire of itself and everyone's death diminishes him.

Pugnacious candidate Digong vowed to feed and fatten the fish in Manila Bay with the carcasses of hundreds of thousands of druggies. Piscean tummies would be the graveyard of druggies, who are weak and frail, and need sympathy and rehab, and not time in our stinking overcrowded underfunded rotten jails, with no meaningful rehab programs. An inmate goes in a human being, and may go out a brute, or an animal.

Digong, who suffers from assaults of migraine, to some, may have become our national headache. (Daughter Sara seems to say there's a better policy than honesty, another conceivable migraine-trigger.) He has had to skip certain very recent events because of a headache, affecting many things, such as moods, but not many people may feel bothered in our society in decay. He uses the powerful Fentanyl for his back pain but has withdrawn support for medical marijuana, a proven pain-killer to others. He, with his doctors, should share the pain of the sick and their families. Compassion is a desideratum.

In late 1985, Macoy's kidney doctor, Dr. Potenciano Baccay, talked about the former's ailment, and was terminated with extreme prejudice, kidnapped, salvaged and silenced forever, brutally. Digong's doctors natcherly would not want a similar fate (bound by a nylon cord, stabbed to death with 20 knife wounds, in the van of the murdered National Kidney Foundation veep), leaving it to Dr. Salvatore Fun-nello to assure the public that the Prez has no major health issue. But, contortionist comedian Sal is not even a horse doctor.

Tomorrow, health issues allowing (I remain basically day-to-day), I plan to make a sentimental journey home to one of my alma maters, the University of Negros Occidental-Recoletos in Bacolod (UNO-R, plain UNO in my time there). There, I had my freshman law and edited the school paper in 1959-60. I had obtained my AB in 1959 in San Beda, where I returned for sophomore law, in 1960, to our 1963 graduation.

My Daddy was helping supervise the engineering aspect of the concreting of the Bacolod airport. We lived at the construction site, in a ramshackle structure. After evening class, I worked as a security guard assisting a Caviteño (Mang Fred Santos, and a lagalag from Taytay, Rizal), and was promoted to night checker of sand and gravel deliveries (checker was my Capitol Hills golf course 1962 summer job also. between my junior and senior law in San Beda - having been promoted from planting grass - PDEA, talaga pong damo, ha?; in senior law, and after the 1963 bar exam, I worked as a full-time messenger in the law firm of Dean Feliciano Jover Ledesma, for baon and merienda).

UNO's Prof. Tuting (or Tutay?) Kilayko was the source of a speech intro that could get me into trouble today. He said a good talk should be like a good bathing suit, long enough to cover the subject and short enough to be interesting. In the early 80's I tried that line in the U.S. and was gently chided and counselled by a feminist, to avoid it. I considered myself told, until today. An atavistic relapse. Sorry.

Atty. Joe Montalbo, Jr. was my Bacolod civil law teacher, who, along with others, validated what Henry Brooks Adams said, that a teacher affects eternity; he never knows where his influence stops. Our Newsette Faculty Adviser was gentle, able and pert Tita Hojilla from Maryknoll, about my age, and when the ed-in-chief left within the schoolyear, I took over. I understand she became a nun and passed away in Latin America. Prof. Arsenio(?) Acuña, from Laguna, I recall, told our class in criminal law that if we mastered the first 21 articles of the Revised Penal Code, that was all we needed to know.

I was astounded that the college song in UNO-R, the Blue and the Gold, was identical to San Beda's the Red & the White. Our class took part in a Glee Club contest and I cannot forget how hard we trained to belt out Stout-Hearted Men.

So much for nostalgia. (I had to narrate above, just in case I am unable to fly out to Bacolod tomorrow, and to replicate the war stories Mon Tulfo and Manong Emil Jurado wrote last Tuesday on their proletarian past.)

Our fighting Prez must learn to heal, not kill. He should avoid saying, "[d]apat nga kayo ang pagbabarilin, " apostrophizing priests.

He should not underrate the powerful effect of rhetoric on human conduct. King Henry II wondered aloud who would rid him of a turbulent priest. And Canterbury Archbishop

Thomas Becket was sent to the Promised Land by four knights who had considered themselves told.

Less divisive prattling, more unifying healing, a consummation devoutly to be wished. Hindi po sana kunsumisyon, generated by our national migraine, father and daughter. Digong should not try to be better than PNoy and all the way of Quezon. Rather, he should heed what iconic Coach John Wooden learned from his father, an Indiana farmer: "Don' t try to be better than somebody else, but never cease trying to be the best you can be."

As I fantasize with my students - that we may never cease to dream. It helps, like legendary John Wooden, to be able to say: "Like my Father, Mother placed her faith in the Good Lord and they taught us to do the same."

Sara, please listen to Mama, and pass on to Papa. I want you to succeed, in giving our people a better life, by the grace of a Compassionate Providence.

Saguisag & Associates Lawyers 4045 Bigasan Street, Palanan 1235 Makati Office Nos. (+632) 551-6350/833-4140 Fax No. (+632) 831-2276

oooooo

15
The second Fall of Bataan?

ARTICLE BY <u>RENE SAGUISAG</u>
MARCH 15, 2019

ALL quiet on the Bataan nuke plant front. But, one never knows when our protean proud and profane Prez may just say gogogo! — given the pro-operation, full-court press of Energy Secretary Alfonso Cusi. I do not question the bona fides of anyone; all mean well, but I remain concerned about a possible second Fall of Bataan.

Last Sunday's Washington Post (thank you, Fil-Am lawyer Chuck Medel) reported on relevant prudential considerations, leading with: "As Japan's leader, Junichiro Koizumi backed nuclear power. Now he's a major foe." Chuck and I went to Wyoming to look at the Balangiga Bells, an issue on which the Prez and I were on the same page. I hope my luck extends to nuke power (on which, more below). We never will, on human rights, sadly. And not on China, either.

Our *wala-naman-tayong-laban* Prez should realize that while China is a dangerous enemy, it is perhaps more dangerous as a friend, to borrow from Georges Clemenceau, who also said that America has miraculously gone from barbarism to decadence without the usual interval of civilization. I would have thought we had two years, 1986 to 1987, as our one brief shining moment as a people.

Next time Digong shakes hands with Xi, he should count his fingers afterwards, while recalling Mactan, Tirad Pass, Bataan and Bessang Pass. Better to die on one's feet than live in shame on bended knees. Why can't we be like the Cubans and Somalis that the Kanos couldn't defeat? Or the Vietnamese whom the French, Kanos and Chinese couldn't, either? It's all about puso.

On public morality, Manong Emil Jurado wrote last Tuesday: "I have been a journalist for a long time and I have never seen as many immoral leaders as I do now." He has been around for almost a century (or two? he sounds that wise). Digong's ratings soar, which may indicate how low we have fallen. E.g., what he says about women and the clergy, as meyor OK lang, di po bagay kung pangulo (with daughter Sara pronouncing that dishonesty is the better policy).

Anyway, back to the nuke plant and the Washington Post report:

"Koizumi has come out of retirement to join a battle against the entrenched business and political interests he had tangled with in the past. [His] new simple catch phrase: `Zero nuclear power.'

"Eight years after the March 11, 2011, nuclear meltdown at the Fukushima Daiichi Nuclear Power Plant, [he] is back in the spotlight, trying to harness the public's growing distrust of such power and rid his country of an industry he once promoted as prime minister from 2001 to 2006.

"A February 2018 poll by Japan's Asahi Shimbun newspaper found 61 percent of respondents against the nation's nuclear plants being restarted and 27 percent in support. `Momentum is building,' he said. `It's only a matter of time.' [He] says he has learned from his mistakes. But Japan's establishment remains firmly behind nuclear plants, even as other critics often point out the dangers posed by Japan's quakes and tsunamis, a word Japan gave the world. `[W]e can turn crisis into opportunity. We can manage ourselves with renewables,' he said. `Take Germany, for example. They saw the disaster in Japan and changed their energy policy...[Japan and Germany are major leaguers, we, *salimpusa*. – RAVS]

"Japan shut down all of its 54 reactors after Fukushima. Explosions in three reactors sent a cloud of radioactive dust across vast swaths of northeastern Japan and forced 165,000 people to flee their homes. But since Shinzo Abe was reelected prime minister in 2012, his government has been on a mission to get the nuclear power industry back on its feet. Nine reactors have already been restarted, six more applications to restart have been approved by a new, nominally independent Nuclear Regulation Authority, and the government wants nuclear power to contribute 20 percent to 22 percent of the nation's energy by 2030. Japan's nuclear agency and the Ministry of Economy, Trade and Industry (METI) say safety standards have been significantly tightened. The aim, said Daisuke Matsuno, director of METI's nuclear energy policy planning division, is to make the industry 'the world's safest.' At the same time, it is dangerous to think you can achieve zero risk. 'Overconfidence is dangerous. Indeed, overconfidence was Japan's downfall.'

"A damning report by an independent parliamentary panel in 2012 concluded that the Fukushima disaster was 'profoundly man-made,' caused by a disregard of the risks of earthquakes by an industry determined to preserve the illusion that nuclear power was absolutely safe. Instead of supervising the industry, METI colluded with it, the report said. It said the risks were downplayed in a culture of 'reflexive obedience' and a 'reluctance to question authority.' (The regulator captured by the regulated, so, what else is new? – RAVS)

"A million tons of contaminated water must be stored, possibly for years, at Japan's Fukushima power plant. METI and Tokyo Electric Power (Tepco), its operator, should have been profoundly embarrassed by those conclusions, Koizumi said, but instead appears unfazed. 'I am stunned. I think they are crazy. Everyone at METI and Tepco are all smart. They all did well in school. Still they don't get it, they don't get how this is costing so much money and is so risky,' he added. So why are elected politicians so determined to press ahead? The answer, [he] asserted, lies in those same vested interests he has spent the best part of his career fighting. Building nuclear power plants is hugely expensive and involves large swaths of industry, which in turn supports the ruling party, [he] said. Labor unions eyeing jobs from nuclear power support the opposition parties, most of whom had backed nuclear power in the past.

"'Nuclear power is behind both sides,' he said. Since 2011, the opposition has swung into the antinuclear camp. But Koizumi has found his own Liberal Democratic Party — also the party of Abe — harder to sway. So much money has also been invested in the industry that there is a reluctance to write investments off. But [he] says nuclear power is neither economic nor necessary. The country, he noted, survived without it for two years without a single blackout.

"[His] journey to the 'zero nuclear' camp began on the day the Fukushima plant ruptured. In retirement, he has devoured books on the subject, and has come to the belief that the world had next to no provisions to safely store nuclear waste.

"Public pressure and litigation in Japan have delayed or prevented several plants from restarting, but critics say risks from earthquakes and volcanic eruptions are still being systematically downplayed…[He] says he has told Abe to embrace renewable energy. 'If Japan went in that direction, the world would look at us differently, with more respect,' he said. 'We can become a model.'

"Other voices of criticism struggle to be heard. Shigeaki Koga, an energy industry expert, says his career was sidelined at METI after he expressed doubts about the safety of nuclear power; he was ultimately forced to resign but has since emerged as a leading public critic. Kunihiko Shimazaki, one of Japan's leading seismologists, warned of the risks of earthquakes and tsunamis along the country's northeast coast for years before the disaster struck, but his reports were generally ignored or buried. After March 2011, he served for two years with the nuclear regulator, and spoke out forcefully, but his term was not renewed. For now, Koizumi is leading the charge and trying to appeal directly to the Japanese people...As someone who believes he was deceived by the nuclear power lobby during his time as prime minister, he sees it as his duty.

"Just as Confucius said, for someone not to correct themselves after making a mistake – that is a true mistake."

Digong should make certain midterm course corrections, on many fronts. *Napapanahon nang maging Pangulo, di na po meyor lang.* Friar lands talk would be useless in Bataan (where the Catholic Church has prudently scrapped funeral mass fees, per this paper yesterday: moot, if the Weapon of Mass Destruction that is the nuke plant melts down, in a country where administration Senate bets, again, are said to believe that dishonesty is the better policy. **Values meltdown**. –

ooooo

16
VICTOR'S JUSTICE AND SPOILS; A PROBLEM LIKE MARIA

MTGIF2/22/19
Manila times opinion
<opinion@manilatimes.net>

When Digong celebrates the birth anniversary of her fave partner, Honeylet, no place in the country would do. Over the weekend, the family had to go Hong Kong to jubilate. How much does it cost us in values (to Jurassics like me, marriage is a sacred institution arguably affected negatively by flaunting a partner, in anything but far from discreet and prudent fashion) and in money? I assume his medical and security personnel also form part of his entourage. Unpardonable to be sure to let the nuke presidential family travel and arguably, junket, by its lonesome.

And then, to the 2016 poll victor belongs the spoils (a Palace caravan in Europe at public expense explaining a journalist's arrest, another arguable junket; may *pinamamarisan ang mga katutubong Gitano?*). And then there's victor's justice, reflecting the prevailing power situation.

The execution of General Tomoyuki Yamashita seems to be a case of such justice, of which we are reminded at this time of year. As we mark another month of the Battle of Manila from February 3 to March 3, 1945, there is a series of poignant retelling of the unspeakable atrocities that then occurred if only because James Scott has come out with MacArthur, Yamashita and the Battle of Manila. I bought a copy of it yesterday.

But, when we took up In Re Yamashita in class in Harvard Law in 1967, I got the impression that the teacher, Prof. Detlev Vagst, was sympathetic to Yamashita. I reacted passionately, or emotionally, if you will, saying that the Japanese General had it coming as Japan had no business invading us in the first place. To my surprise, my classmates of about a hundred in the huge ampitheatre where we were having class, burst into spontaneous applause. So young and impetuous, we all were.

It took decades for me to understand why Catholic Justice Frank Murphy, the last American Governor General here - after whom what is now Camp Aguinaldo was known in my youth - sharply dissented. He wrote that "the high feelings of the moment doubtless will be satisfied but in the sober afterglow will come the realization of the boundless and dangerous implications of the procedure sanctioned today. The [atrocities] do not justify the abandonment of our devotion to justice in dealing with a fallen enemy commander."

As columnist Mon Farolan wrote last February 11 in the Inquirer, the ruling has come to be known as the Yamashita Standard (or the Medina Standard, after Capt. Medina in Vietnam) for Command Responsibility. History is written by the victors, who render a brand of justice reflective of their triumph.

But, Murphy warned: "At a time like this [early 1946] when emotions are understandably high it is difficult to adopt a dispassionate attitude toward a case of this nature. Yet now is precisely the time when that attitude is most essential. While peoples in other lands may not share our beliefs as to due process and the dignity of the individual, we are not free to give effect to our emotions in reckless disregard of the rights of others. . . . Indeed, an uncurbed spirit of revenge and retribution, masked in formal legal procedure for purposes of dealing with a fallen enemy commander, can do more lasting harm than all of the atrocities giving rise to that spirit."

And Yamashita was hanged in February 1946.

Whatever may be the rule in actual shooting war situations involving combatants, such as whether Bill Clinton should be liable in the failed 1993 Black Hawk Down sortie in

Somalia, I believe he should account and answer only to history. I have little difficulty accepting the concept of command responsibility in case of gross human rights violations victimizing unarmed non-combatants.

The U.S. 9th Circuit Court of Appeal, in Hilao v. Estate of Marcos said, in 1995, in the human class suit against the Marcoses, that "there is little question that Marcos caused tremendous harm to many people." Unlike Yamashita who had lost control of his trapped troops, Marcos was super-executive, super-court, super-legislature and a one-man continuing constitutional convention. Totally in command and control.

Was PNoy in such a situation when the Mamasapano 64 were killed (not just the 44 heroes, I always include the score or so Muslim victims, including Sara, 5, killed, and her parents, wounded, and the slain Muslim farmer whose eyes were gouged out - dinukit - Muslim lives also matter)? Permit me to doubt while we await another James Scott to come up with another opus on that successful effort to nail down international terrorist Marwan. Cup, three-fourths- full, in my view. Fortunes of war. PNoy may be accountable to history, but not liable. We need a new voice which won't just echo what our militarized or "police- sized" bureaucracy says.

A voice, not an echo, is Manong JPE, who doesn't see federalism as making money grow on trees. It is silly of course to say "I am corrupt because we aren't federal." JPE was Senate Prez when R.A. No. 10175 became law in late 2012.

I find disconcerting the application of this relatively new law to Maria Ressa, namely, An Act Defining Cybercrime, Providing for the Prevention, Investigation, Suppression and the Imposition of Penalties Therefor and for Other Purposes.

Sec. 26(1) of the Constitution says "[e]very bill passed by the Congress shall embrace only one subject which shall be expressed in the title thereof," to warn us of what may come.** The title, to me, did not alert the people that defamation would be treated more harshly if done in cyberspace (I, jurassic, email and read widely but cannot do facebook, viber, netfix, etc., to save my life). Ergo, unconstitutional, arguably. Cyber may have limited reach compared to newspapers and radio-TV. So, why harsher?

Buatis v. People shows the humane and libertarian trend of Supreme Court decisions on free speech. There a lawyer was labelled as "lousy, inutil, [inflicting] carabao English, stupid[ity] and satan") , which merited for the utterer in the end only a fine of 6,000.00, with the prison sentence deleted by the High Court. No jail time for an utterance even if the offended lawyer was subjected "to public ridicule as even his own family have told him `Ginagawa ka lang gago dito'," 485 SCRA 275, 287 (2006).

Like cases, like treatment. More speech, not less. Falsehood is fought in the sunlight, a good disinfectant, with truth, not jail. Only heavy damage awards should be inflicted as a deterrent. The appellate courts have established a trend of no jail time, only fines in libel, given the value of free speech. If Congress would want to reverse it, the public should be forewarned in a bill's title - and heard.

Maria Ressa's true crime is being critical of the Prez. She cannot be above the law. She should not be below it, either.

Are we seeing an administration- inspired revolt against the judicial humanitarian and libertarian standard in free speech cases? This is no way to solve a problem like Maria. Dual citizen? I have clients seeking such a status for its benefits, but of course. Nothing sinister about it.

On lawmaking, to set the record straight on Maharlika, Kuya Eddie Ilarde, my fellow ex-Senator, texted that Macoy in fact never proposed renaming our country Maharlika. My long-time and valued pal, whose Parang Kahapon Lamang won't ever be beyond easy recall ("nagtampisaw sa batis ng kaligayahan, " "at nangyari ang dapat mangyari," atbp.), recalled that in filing a bill so renaming our country, "Imelda who was a member of Congress [the Batasan] never supported it." Marcos could have done it by decree but never did, Kuya Eddie stressed.

Did Macoy realize that the Perlas ng Silangan might have been called Phallus-Pinas? Or Pili-Penis?

Meanwhile, goodbye and thank you, fellow Bedan Bobby Manosa, a National Artist, gone to a better world, with Frisco San Juan, an authentic WWII hero with the genuine Hunters, not the fake Maharlika. Thank you Dr. Louie Kodumal, for your lecture last Monday in San Beda's college of medicine and donation of P1M for scholarships.

And Manny Pacquiao is right in aping Muhammad Ali who told TV host Dick Cavett on whether he'd advise a kid to go into the manly art of modified murder, something like - "listen, man, the chances of making it are a million to one; it's too dangerous, go to school, be a doctuh, be a lawyuh, be a mechanic," etc., which rolled trippingly from the tongue.

On whether Sara should succeed Digong in 2022, would that not circumvent the ban on reelection? GMA and PNoy had to wait for decades to supervene and therefore could not use government resources in a paradise of pedigree. The spirit, not the letter.

Saguisag & Associates Lawyers 4045 Bigasan Street, Palanan 1235 Makati Office Nos. (+632) 551-6350/833-4140 Fax No. (+632) 831-2276

oooooo

17
LEI-LA PASIONARIA; MAHARLIKA?

MTGIF2-15-19
Manila times opinion
opinion@manilatimes.net

Senator Leila de Lima reminds me of that tough Basque heroine, Dolores Ibarruri, La Pasionaria. They may have differing ideologies but when it comes to courage, principle, work ethic and eloquence, Leila more than qualifies as our own La Pasionaria, who cried during the Spanish civil war No Pasaran! They shall not pass, manifesting undiscourageable resolute resistance.

Bedan bar topnotcher (No. 8) Lei-La Pasionaria needs our support and prayers in the face of seemingly creeping militarization, where even the DSWD (Department of Social Welfare & Development) is now oddly headed by a retired general. The military is now equal, if not superior, to civilian authority, not the original understanding under the Constitution, as I perceive it.

Superior, at least, in terms of more benefits, which all public servants of course deserve, to accentuate the unnecessary; however, it seems the President continues to feel insecure. But, for him not to worry, in this land of party animals, we'd rather party, text and selfie/Kodakan. Digong continues to be fond of the Nazi salute, with the clenched right fist thrust forward, identified with Hitler, and aped by fawning frightened or innocent/ignorant guests.

A coup is not in the cards, from where I sit. Ninoy Aquino likened the Pinoy to the carabao, slow to anger (but once it does, watch out, as in 1986, after nearly 14 years, with Digong's mother a a prime mover in Davao).

If Leila had been quiet, or even "prudently&quo t; voiced support to the regime, she should not be in a small cage now, but with us, the dissenters asking foolish questions, in a wider cage in which to roam. It has been said that those who begin the coercive elimination of dissent soon find themselves exterminating dissenters; the compulsory unification of opinion only leads to the unanimity of the graveyard. - Justice Robert Jackson. Take a bow, Maria Ressa, another gutsy victim of coercive elimination of dissent.

True, Leila is an addict, a human rights addict, like Ka Pepe Diokno - whose son, Dean Chel, belongs in the Senate; he, along with Erin Tanada, Pilo Hilbay, Neri Colmenares, Samira Gutoc, et al., holds the passed torch of human rights advocacy, at which the President sadly looks askance. Ka

Pepe was not even charged despite being detained for two years. She is charged and caged (ibon mang may layang lumipad) for an implausible nonexistent offense. Kenkoy case, I submit, as in the case of Hubert Webb, where druggie Jessica Alfaro, in NBI custody, could be, and was, made to sing any song for her supper.

Hubert & Co. wasted more than 15 years in jail given the pervasive prejudicial publicity we had to contend with; as his original temporary lawyer, I cried from the start that I'd carry to my grave that Hubert was thousands of miles away when the Vizconde Massacre occurred on June 30, 1991. (Here, Mon Tulfo, Winnie Monsod, Teddy Benigno and I formed an unlikely barbershop quartet.) Mario Ongkiko (late), the Webbs' first choice as counsel but who was then tied up, and Met Custodio, tirelessly carried and soldiered on - to a fair and right conclusion. But, unjust detention even for a second, is torment beyond compare. Hubert & Co., 15+ years.

Lei-La Pasionaria was arrested on February 24, 2017 and will mark her second anniversary in a cage next week.

Hail Leila. No pasaran! - of which I am also reminded when dealing with our traffic which seems to get worse every day. We hardly move and cannot pass (unlike motorcycles in the millions, it seems, like ants).

Last Sunday, I, driver-less, walked about half a kilometer from our Bigasan, Palanan, Makati home to pay my last respects to Msgr. Antero Aure Sarmiento, in St. Joseph the Worker Church, where he had served. He always found the time for small talk after the services as my late wife, Dulce and I, would attend the 6:00 p.m. daily Mass every chance we got. May I also extend my condolences to the family of iconic Armida Siguion Reyna, who I'd see ballroom dancing in Bahia in Intercon, now demolished.

After Mass last Sunday, I took two tricycles (the first quit) to go to Cash N Carry to take a cab for Resorts World. A Dance Instructor (DI) I had booked texted that at four p.m. she started waiting for a bus in Bacoor, Cavite but gave up at six cuz she could not get a ride. That is the transport situation today for commuters and others even if the weather is fair. Absolutely nothing to gloat about here.

For another instance, last Friday, I left the Office of the City Prosecutor in Paranaque at 1:30 p.m. but got to the NLRC (National Labor Relations Commission) on Banawe, Quezon City more than two hours later. Yup, the situation today, gridlock in Nagtahan, same in España, etc.. When I got there, I was told that the Arbiter concerned had taken ill.

Traffic sickens, a fave excuse of my tardy students, which may even be occasionally true.

Lei-La-Pasionaria has a lot to gripe about, along with millions of commuters, wasting/spending a quarter or more of their daily lives travelling. Metro Manila might soon stand still. Does Malacanang care? It seems to agree that traffic is like the weather, per Mark Twain, everyone talks about it but does little or nothing sa bansang matiisin aside from administration bragging.

As Ninoy Aquino would intone in repetition, better to die on one's feet, than live in shame on bended knees. In various forms it is attributed to Benito Juarez and Emiliano Zapata of Mexico and Spain's La Pasionaria, who said: "antes morir de pie que vivir de rodillas." Their preference: to die proudly on one's feet to living in shame on bended knees, my own embroidered recasting.

Lei-La Pasionaria's Dispatch from Crame last Saturday, on the ordeal of Col. Ferdinand Marcelino, said she was glad that he had "found the courage to speak out and assert anew his innocence on the drug charges previously filed against him. . . . I know exactly, without any exaggeration, how it feels to be falsely accused. Perhaps what many people do not know is the previously dismissed charges against Col. Marcelino were then revived in order to pressure him to falsely testify against me. . . . [A long line of convicted criminals was recruited as perjured] witnesses against me in exchange for privileges and special treatment, and for them to stay alive.]

Better to suffer and die on one's feet than live in shame on bended knees. Col. Marcelino refused to be a Jessica Alfaro but the Palace found many jailbirds, canaries willing to sing its song, its own Jessicas.

Digong has another maleficent obsession, renaming our country after Maharlika, to honor fake war hero Marcos and his phony guerilla unit. Scholarship should conclusively establish first beyond cavil that Maharlika does not in fact stand for a giant phallus.

Is Digong serious in renaming our country? Can the Pinoy live up to its supposed meaning and rise to the occasion? As may be seen in UP's annual Oblation run? Do we need reminding that Macoy was a fake hero whose supposed exploits were made from whole cloth?

North and South America do not seem to mind having been named after Italian Amerigo Vespucci.

But, given the reported P99B-pork of lawmakers, why not rename our whole archipelago as the Babuyan Islands?

Ladrones Islands is spoken for (now Marianas). And we can rename LMB as Libingan ng Isang Mandarambong at Berdugo, at mga Bayani (LIMBB), spoken for.

Saguisag & Associates Lawyers4045 Bigasan Street, Palanan1235 MakatiOffice Nos. (+632) 551-6350/833-4140 Fax No. (+632) 831-2276

oOOOOOo

18
MANNY PACQUIAO:
SENATE DESAPARECIDO

MTGIF1/18/19
Manila Times Editorial
<newsdesk@manilatimes.net>

I associate myself with the reported 66% per cent of our people polled, expressing concern over Digong's health, not satisfied with Dr. Sal Panelo's inexpert clearance. My pal, Compañero Sal, is not even a horse doctor, I don't think. A panel of real doctors may examine Digong, and if he consents, report to the nation. Adamantine refusal heightens our solicitude or anxiety. We don't need a Marcos situation redux; Macoy suffered in secrecy while we suffered openly. More transparency we seek - and deserve. We have the human right to know. A Prez is public property, certainly on health issues.

I wish Prez Digong good health with the wish that he would make certain midterm course corrections. Such as being Pangulo, sa halip na Meyor lang, and not wasting/spending his time in petty senseless quarrels, say, with women ("shoot them in the vagina" , "rape comes with the territory" , etc.) and the Catholic Church.

So what if there are gays in my Church? This goes for gays everywhere, as long as they try their best to do good and avoid evil in our uncertain, less than perfect world. Alexander the Great, Michelangelo, Lawrence of Arabia and Rock Hudson were said to be gays but the world owes them. Even sinners, and we all are, we owe. We have St. Augustine and St. Mary Magdalene. Meyor Digong wastes/spends a lot of time dividing us and even endangering our women by saying that rape is part of alien culture. Bahala na po ba sila sa buhay nila?

Senator Manny Pacquiao is said to unite the nation when he fights. Hmmmm. He cannot answer when the roll is called this week as Congress resumes work. He contended for Top House Absentee and only a few noticed in the Bigger House. But, in the Better House, they are only 24 (23, with Gringo Honasan gone, for a Cabinet post?). An empty Senate seat glares.

Manny should read and take to heart Sec. 4 of R.A. No. 6713 which mandates that he, as a public official, must always uphold public interest over and above personal interest, perform and discharge his duties with the highest degree of excellence, professionalism, intelligence and skill, show utmost devotion and dedication to duty, and shall not indulge in extravagant and ostentatious display of wealth in any form.

Would I be the only Pinoy who won't watch him on Sunday in his seemingly insatiable quest for more fame and fortune? Am I the only Pinoy bothered by his excrescent neglect of Senate work and his disrespectful and questionable, even cockamamie, priorities?

In the manly art of modified murder (W.O. McGeehan), Manny should forget Mayweather and focus on the problems caused by the bad weather in places many back home, for just one national concern or problem.

Or he should resign to pursue more fame and fortune, to enable him to settle his tax issues in the billions reportedly. He may be our Top Tax Evader or Avoider. His secret weapon: brown-nose Prez Duterte or else get the Maria Ressa treatment.

Do we still have a Senate ethics panel?

From 1987 to 1992, Manong Ernie Maceda and I were never late, much less absent, in the Senate. Non sibi, sed patriae. Not self, but country. Kapakanang Pambayan, di po pansarile. Is this principle dead in the water in our decaying society headed by our proud and profane president? In North America, we hear "pobre Mejico, tan lejos de Dios y tan cerca de Estados Unidos." Poor Mexico, so far from God and so near the United States." Here, "Pobre Filipinas, tan lejos de estupido dios y tan cerca de China.." Roughly, poor Philippines, so far from Digong's stupid god, and so near his beloved China.

A recent poll show that Pinoys prefer the U.S. to China; we don't hear of Pinoys clamoring for immigrant visas to live up north in the Middle Kingdom.

Anyway, I wish Manny and his Wassisname foe good luck in not getting hurt seriously. Studies show how getting in the head viciously affects one's well-being and may conduce to overreaching beyond his limitations. There's CTE, chronic traumatic encephalopathy to worry about.

Now, we know that Senator Bong Revilla intends to return to the Senate (with comebacking Lito Lapid) and the Metro Manila Film Festival in 2019, also for fame and fortune.

Who will mind the store, as it were, in the All-Star Senate, on the West Philippine Sea, Sabah, budget insertions, anti-poor war on drugs, massive worsening poverty situation, widespread homelessness and starvation, insurgency, jail overcrowding, traffic, pollution, etc.? One of the hardest working Senators has been Leila de Lima, a jewel, even in jail, working for the least, lost and last, for whom we are asked to pray.

Pobre Filipinas. Bong and Lito should just go to the Bigger House for sectoral showbiz representation unless they expand their horizons, which I am sure they can be capable of. Bong has just been acquitted by a divided Sandiganbayan, inviting criticism.

All Senators may fantasize and consider themselves as presidential timber, as has been said of Manny Pacquiao (with Mocha Uson as possible Veep? - another joke?). But first they must rise to the mantle of Senatorship. And Meyor Digong must rise to the mantle of his office, of being Pangulo, as was said of petty Master Tweeter Donald Trump, by new U.S. Senator Mitt Romney.

The mantle may include the Manila Bay clean-up. But, why doesn't the Palace, Manila, Makati and Pasay first clean up the Tripa de Gallina estero near where I live, which may not be as sexy as Boracay, but just because I am such a nice guy? A far more do-able goal. And *cosas pequeñas significan mucho*, little things mean a lot.

Saguisag & Associates Lawyers 4045 Bigasan Street, Palanan 1235 Makati Office Nos. (+632) 551-6350/833-4140 Fax No. (+632) 831-2276

ooooooo

19
NOT CHARTER, BUT CHARACTER, CHANGE

MTGIF1-4-19
Manila times opinion
<opinion@manilatimes.net>

For 2019, I wish people would always text me ahead to ask if they could call. It used to be calls would be coursed through office or> household staff, which helped if I was in the middle of something truly urgent screaming for focused attention. Also, if one greeting me during the holiday season would identify oneself. Memory deteriorating in my second adolescence, oooops, childhood pala. So, to the Does who greeted me during the season of grace and goodwill, thank you very very many, haha.

Lawmakers offered P30M to solve the ruthless Batocabe murder (my condolences) , with Digong adding 20M. From their own pockets? More likely, from public funds. What then was the legal basis? Under the Origination Clause, all appropriation measures must originate exclusively in the House, to be concurred in by the Senate. Const., Art. VI, Sec. 4. Thus, Congress, not the Executive, has the power of the purse. But, the Prez appropriates right and left with the cuckolded Congress not questioning the seeming usurpation of power.

Not only that, he even creates offices, a legislative power as it involves appropriation. If ad hoc or temporary, maybe he deserves a free pass; but, in the spirit of transparency, how much has such an exercise cost us as in the Presidential Initiative (PI-1, for concision) for charter change? PI I associate only with People's Initiative under Sec.. 32 of Art.

VI of the Constitution, which is silent on the Digong's PI-1. Is it imbedded in one of the great silences of the Constitution, as empowering a sitting Prez to use it to promote certain narrow self-interests? A Prez needs to be protected from himself. PI-1s in the past bit the dust, but utterly.

I have also long wondered about the legality of the seemingly permanent Presidential Anti-Crime Commission (PACC), which only our pindeho Congress can create. This creation may be another instance of presidential overreach. It duplicates what the DOJ, PNP, NBI and the Ombudsman do. Even Congress, acting purportedly in aid of legislation, not prosecution; there, a resource person's counsel is not much more than part of the furniture. A suspect in a police stationhouse is supposed to be told "you have a right to remain silent, to counsel, etc.". The Bill of Rights is checked at the congressional gate.

In the U.S., one loses the right not to speak on a prior ironclad guarantee of immunity granted by some court, which makes sense, but I fear our pindeho lawmakers cannot tell "transactional " or "use" immunity from a hole in the ground. Or simply do not care.

I hope presidential overreach won't extend to the reported revival of the mothballed Bataan nuke power plant, which to me is beyond economic repair (I chaired the Cabinet and Senate Committees on it). Obsolete 70's technology it is based on; cheaper to build a new one from the ground up (as in choosing between renovating or building a new one altogether). But where? NIMBY, Not in My Back Yard, baby.

With all due respect, do we have the people and the technology that the U.S., Russia and Japan have, in dealing with the 1979 Three Mile Island, the 1986 Chernobyl and the 2012 Fukushima disasters, respectively? In none of these countries do they, I think, have weird superhighways which end in a one-lane portion. I travel every Saturday between San Beda Law Mendiola and San Beda Law Alabang; when we get into the one-lane phase after the Alabang toll plaza to get to Zapote, I pray hard for my old vehicle not to make tirik. The cusses I'd get from those behind me would make Digong at his most colorful, sound like an angelic altar boy. Accidents waiting to happen our technical people arrange. The administration must work hard to sell nuke power.

And what is this RFID (radio frequency identification) system where certain motorists get privileged treatment? Why not simply widen toll plazas as in Balintawak so everyone equally benefits? Unwarranted privilege is a form of anti-poor corruption.

On reducing corruption, prosecution won't do it. We have to follow what they do elsewhere. Work out compensation packages that put the government worker above the level of temptation and corruption, not only for cops and soldiers. The Pinoys who work in those countries are paid well, cum good health care and pension programs. They behave. Graft has been with mankind for thousands of years, despite the Ten Commandments, but appreciably lower in countries with superior working conditions. Man normally would rather be honest than otherwise.

What really deters is not the severity of the penalty but swift and certain conviction. If crooks are convicted and jailed within a year or two, that would affect human conduct under the supermarket theory of the criminal law. If unaffordable, given speedy justice and our horrid prison conditions, the market principle would prevail and deter.

What can PACC do with the law's delay? It can only refer its pro-Digong output to another body. Again, take the Lenny Villa frat hazing death on February 11, 1991. I represented Zos Mendoza who, I can tell only in April 2016, that hardworking and shabbily-treated Chief Justice Meilou Sereno ended the case after 25 years.

What can the PACC do in the matter of subtle corruption or unethical conduct? Such as why is senatorial candidate Bong Go getting, to me, prodigious unprecedented publicity? Full page ads on how lucky we are to have him around. Obscene. Garapal, in my view. Is this any way of elevating our ethical standards now in decay? The Comelec seems inutile here.

Senator Manny Pacquiao gets a ton of publicity, not for any sterling senatorial initiative but in gaining more billions on which his income taxes payment continues to be hazy. But, the acclaimed boxer is seen to make sipsip to the Prez, guaranteeing immunity. The BIR goes after acclaimed Maria Ressa whose clear crime is being a critic. I wish Manny and Wassisname good luck on January 19 in that neither gets severely battered in the head. We need clear-thinking Senators. One study of the American Association of Neurologial Surgeons shows that 90% of boxers suffer serious brain damage in the manly art of modified murder (W.O. McGeehan). Manny should be concerned about our bad weather and not focus on baiting Floyd Mayweather, Jr. for another big-bucks fight. Or he may resign now as Senator as the decent, honorable thing to do. The Senate is not a sideline or hobby.

More than charter change, what we need is character change. Good people change others, better people change the system, the best ones change themselves. This I paraphrase from Leo Tolstoy' s "[e]veryone thinks of changing the system but no one thinks of changing himself." And Alexander Pope wrote, "for forms of government let fools contest, whate'er is best administered is best."

Superlawyer Gerry Spence reminds us that something shines in almost all of us. Even for the Ateneo bully, who, like Digong of Ateneo de Davao, and Erap, of Ateneo de Manila, may yet, as one in conflict with the law or school norms, become President someday.

Digong's high poll rating is compatible with the rise of pussy-grabber Donald Duck Trump and Brazil's ungallant Jair Bolsinaro ("I won't rape you because you don't deserve it"} in a world in seeming decay.

Good manners and right conduct continue to get battered in a world in putrefaction. I hope and pray that in the remaining years of Digong as Prez he will arrest the decay here. The youth, the hope of the Motherland, cannot have as a model our profane Prez. He's fast ruining our values with his "jokes, " a lame excuse of funny man Sal Panelo.

Yes, character - not charter - change we need. My wish then for this year is for Digong to metamorphose from Meyor to President, beginning with his language. As it is, he sets a bad example. To illustrate, hooliganism our infected cage team inflicted while hosting Australia during the FIBA qualifiers match last July. Coach Chot Reyes was fined P536,000 for urging his players to "hit somebody." And Samahang Basketbol ng Pilipinas was asked to pay P13M.

Shall we try to return to civility this year?

To be groped as a poor exploited maid may explain why she (or a brother of hers) might join the NPA. The Meyor's thoughtless response: shoot her in the vagina. Dividing, not unifying. And time to junk his hazy ontological exegesis on theology. The Meyor was not elected to be Pangulo on that divisive basis. Time for a mid-course correction. From Meyor to Pangulo, finally. Sana naman po.

We can have a Party Animal for Prez, singing Ikaw to whoever. No problem there. But, a Panty Animal who talks too much?

Saguisag & Associates Lawyers 4045 Bigasan Street, Palanan 1235 Makati Office Nos. (+632) 551-6350/833- 4140 Fax No. (+632) 831-2276

Oooooo

20
BULLY THE BULLY, RAPE THE RAPIST?

MTGIF12-28-28
Manila times opinion
opinion@manilatimes.net

It has been another challenging year. More so, for those of us in our senior years, aging and ailing. May we all have a better one in 2019, against difficult odds.

I may be in the arguably tiny minority caring for the Ateneo stude, Joaquin Quintos, 14, who may have been destroyed forever. Or at least damaged severely. Nietzsche - who said he considered a day wasted when he didn't dance at least once - is also known for saying that what doesn't destroy one can only make him stronger. Did he also say that he who is merely just, is severe?

Ateneo, it seems to me, was unfairly bullied and panicked into taking posthaste an UnChristian posture at the height of the holiday season. Was the right thing done at the wrong time?

World War I lore has it that one Christmas Eve the Allies and the Germans stopped fighting, and started singing Christmas carols and even played football. Christmas affects the conduct of warriors but not bullied Ateneo?

I counsel my studes to do the Right Thing in the Right Place in the Right Way for the Right Reason at the RIGHT TIME. I would have preferred Ateneo's taking the matter under advisement in the spirit of the season of grace and goodwill; it could merely announced "probe going on" and holding off a decision until the year turned, and not heeding the taunt of those crying "crucify him! crucify him!", long before Lent.

Chesterton said Christianity is neither a success nor a failure for the simple reason that it has never been tried. Christmas was pushed into irrelevance at a trying time. Ateneo was tested, and, from where I humbly sit, found wanting. If the Yuletide spirit does not work there at this time, then when and where?

The hooting - not caroling - throng cried for blood and got it. It might have satisfied the strong feelings of the moment but in the sober afterglow may come the realization of questionable timing; here, I paraphrase Justice Frank Murphy, a devout Catholic and a militant human rights defender, who served as our last American Governor-General (and after whom Camp Aguinaldo was named when I was young long long ago). In sharp dissent, he voted to acquit Yamashita, who had lost contact with, and control of, his troops but was hanged anyway. His father was of the noble Samurai class.

Of course there is the argument against misplaced compassion but who's to say?

Jose P. Laurel, Sr., a kissing bandit (Concepcion Lat was the kissee), was tried for attempted murder for stabbing a rival suitor (Exequiel Castillo) with a balisong on December 26, 1909. On March 15, 1912, the Supreme Court acquitted him. Old Jai Alai patrons will recall el fallo del juez es inapelable. A judge's decision is unappealable. He went on to become President during World War II and an acclaimed accomplished national leader who fathered admirable patriotic progeny.

Just before WWII, Justice Laurel was to write the decision of October 22, 1940 acquitting Ferdinand E. Marcos in the murder case of Julio Nalundasan, who had beaten Mariano Marcos in the 1934 congressional elections. There's a lesson there.(?)

San Beda allowed Digong Duterte to graduate (but not to join the graduation march; in Harvard Law, attendance is absolutely optional; I skipped it in 1968), his having shot classmate Octavio Goco who had taunted him as a promdi, notwithstanding. Digong however failed to accelerate Goco's reporting to our Maker, to sleep in heavenly peace; Goco passed away in the U.S. in 2004 in the U.S. (in this regard, goodbye and thanks, Lorna Verano-Yap, a comrade in the anti-dictatorship struggle).

My recollection of the event out of the long ago is somewhat hazy but two close friends have reminded me of it and my hard-line role in the ensuing disciplinary proceedings. Others not as close have come up with alternative versions, one saying that it was all an accident after all.. But, why was he not allowed to march then?

Talkative Digong noticeably has been quiet about the Ateneo bullying, I suppose given his own colorful past. Weird, had he condemned it. He may not be a bully perhaps in the sense that he may be a Nike "Just Do It" Poster Boy.

So, the issue remains, do we bully the bully? Sounds like rape the> rapist to me.

In Makati Elementary, our principal, disciplinarian Mr. Cortez, would punch us in the tummy aside from allowing other manifestations of the biblical spare-the-rod- spoil-the- child norm. Our brilliant Math teacher in Rizal High, Mr. Valdez, would tell us to go home and plant camote, for our wrong answers. Super Judge (later, Justice) Solidum, our senior year criminal law teacher, heard my reply the first time I was called to recite and blurted: "In this class, Mr. Saguisag, you have to use your brains, if you have any!" Bullying could be oral and just be as challenging or damaging. A law professor of ours so scared the bejesus out of a very bright classmate, assertive to the point of being somewhat of a braggart, whose mind would go blank every time he'd be called to recite; he'd just stand there, speechless. He, gone now, flunked but became a very good lawyer anyway and was with us in MABINI.

Earlier, in our youth on Pasig we engaged in barrio versus barrio fist fights (with the smaller one may hawak, say a piece of wood, as odds equalizer), tirahan (with palara or tin foil) and sword fights (between our leaders; I remember when our Uding once lopped off part of the lip of his foe he dueled with in a narrow gang plank). Our elders bullied us in basketball games, even at tip-off pa lang, sasahurin na, part of our toughening process in this cruel world. One could simply go home of course and sort of miss much of the fun in childhood. We were not babied.

Once, when we were being bullied to give up our basketball slot we had reserved for in the Pasig Convento, for the use of night lights, Belgian Fr. Roger Jolle (CICM - which we then said meant Can I Collect Money?) stood his ground and shooed the bullies away. Lesson learned on standing on principle.

It seems to me the tough love my parents showed in spanking us made us better persons. We'd do more of the misconduct we weren't penalized for. For swimming in Pasig, we'd be taken to the woodshed, as it were. Today, parents may expect a subpoena, with its dirty linen, damaging family relations, deeply, even permanently. Modern views trump the biblical proverb - spare the rod, spoil the child - and reinforce family bonding.

If Ateneo bully Joaquin Quintos reforms and becomes President some day he might yet understand the reason for the season of grace and goodwill. If not of Lent, which teaches suffering, salvation and redemption. Meantime, he is learning that in life, when you laugh, the whole world laughs with you, but you weep, alone.

Well, Al Mendoza, my pal, who I last met in MOA Arena in 2013, in the FIBA Asia cage championship for men, where we shone - if Joaquin Quintos will allow me, I'll walk and weep with him. As a by-and-large lifelong loser myself, I can say, "you' ll never walk and weep alone. I'll walk and weep with you." Here, I may be with Robert Aventajado of the Philippine Taekwondo Association who believes in giving Quintos a second chance. In punishment, there must be equivalence or proportionality and the possibility of change and subjective growth. I have benefited from forgiveness for my many failings.

May I also laud Chief Justice Lucas Bersamin for reminding us in his reported recent visit to the Manila Youth Reception Center that CICLs (Children in Conflict with the Law) deserve a new beginning. The Ateneo bully is but 14, if I may repeat. Also, Education Secretary Liling Briones for likewise seeing the bigger picture.

Bullying the bully sounds too much like raping the rapist. Disproportionate, not fitting the offense.

Have a better year. 2019 is the Year of the Youth for whom we pray and wish the best, with Joaquin Montes, 14, not excluded.

For my part, I will keep asking the foolish questions of the day, and take the less travelled road (Frost), sail against the wind (the Kennedys), march to the beat of a different drummer (Thoreau) and not see things that are and ask - why? but rather see things that never were and ask - why not (Shaw)?

Happy New Year!

Saguisag & Associates Lawyers 4045 Bigasan Street, Palanan 1235 Makati Office Nos. (+632) 551-6350/833-4140 Fax No. (+632) 831-2276

oooooooo

21
BELLS BACK WHERE THEY BELONG

MTIGIF12/14/18
Manila times opinion
<opinion@manilatimes.net>

If Digong's astig or boorish image or style - e.g., saying what he thought of Obama's mother - results in something positive, so does his soft side, in asking that we emulate the Blessed Virgin Mother, whose feast has become a non-working holiday during his watch. (In dance halls, I know blissful virgin mothers, who claim they are not so distant promises of beauty untouched by the world and then they seek my advice on the legal concerns of their love children).

Our palamura Prez convinced the Americans to return the Bells of Balangiga, capping the efforts of many, going back to the last millennium.

In 1974, with Ramon Revilla, Beauty Queen Au Pijuan starred in a movie Sunugin ang Samar indicating that even then the Bells posed issues few might have been aware of.

My own continuing interest in the Bells started in the 80's, in the Senate. In my September 12, 1994 column here, I said I had "heard from Prof. Rolando O. Borrinaga, of UP-Leyte" , who said that the Bells "remind our people about a vicious but forgotten war that cost the lives of more [Warays] than any other conflict in our local history."

"Prof. Borrinaga and I have shared for some time a concern about the . . . long overdue return of the bells and the cannon now sitting in an honored place in Fort Warren just out of charming Cheyenne.

I wrote: "Go there, young man, look at the bells, look at the cannon, look at the inscription, and see if you can be so insensitive as not to feel something surging within you, close to inspiring you to organize a commando raid to return them where they belong."

"Maybe when President Bill Clinton comes a-visiting in November [1994], he can vow I SHALL RETURN - the Bells of Balangiga. It is a possible electrifying talking point, if he can pronounce the place name.

"It is time some focus were applied to the enterprise. Many people off and on have worked on it. Remembrance enables us to have a sense of where we are and should be going. The bells can toll to remind us that there are proud moments in our wretched past, when our people, united, fought for honor and did not behave like a circular firing squad. There may not be too many of them but such a one was one Sunday morning in September 93 Years ago, in a place that does not exactly fall trippingly from the tongue. . . . But, from time to time enough Filipinos agree on what truly matters and we have our Balangigas, Mactans, Bessang Passes and Edsas, when we hear the footsteps of history. . . .

"Let freedom ring once more from those bells, back in Balangiga where they belong, to punctuate America' s generosity of spirit and the gallantry of our forebears, and complete the healing."

In Cheyenne, we [Atenean Chuck Medel and I] met a family from UP, whose patriarch said in jest that UP stood for Useless People, haha. One UP placard last week in Araneta read: "WEST PHL SEA, ATIN 'TO!" Senate-bound Pilo Hilbay had one such sign. Last year, at halftime, Ateneo's Blue Babble Battalion denounced EJKs and the reduction of the Commission on Human Right budget to P1,000. In 2016, they displayed MARCOS NOT A HERO." Way to go. There is hope in the millenials and for the Fatherland.

On September 29, 1993, I wrote here: "YESTERDAY marked the 92nd anniversary of the Massacre of Balangiga, Samar.

"The earliest recorded effort I have seen to get them back was in 1957. My fellow Maubanin, Fr. Horacio de la Costa S.J., wrote twice to Mr. Chip Wards, Command Historian of the 13th Air Force in San Francisco, California. After the year turned, the Franciscan Fathers in Guihulngan, Negros Oriental, also wrote to Mr. Ward, pressing the point that one of the bells was of Franciscan origin.

"As early as 1911, there was a view in the US War Department that it may be appropriate to question the propriety of taking (even as a souvenir) a bell belonging to the Catholic church simply because a recreant native priest either used it or permitted it to be used to sound a signal of attack on American soldiers. The bell belonged to the church and not to the priest." It was not the fault of the church but that of the priest that it was used or misused, if that.

"Last year [1992], in Crow Creek adjoining Cheyenne, Wyoming, I [with Chuck] visited the F.E. Warren Air Force Base. There I saw the two bells (dated 1883 and 1889 respectively) and the British-made Falcon cannon (circa 16th century) brought to America early this century by US soldiers as war trophies."

"There is a lot of support for the return of the bells. The people of Balangiga, the Department of Foreign Affairs, the National Historical Institute, Rep. Joe Ramirez, et al. have worked on it for some years now, off and on. [Cong. Raul Daza stood to applaud the Prez who mentioned the Bells in his State of the Nation Address last year. A forebear of his, Eugenio Daza, was among the leaders in 1901, who designed the plan of attack, with lances, bolos, clubs and daggers.]

"However, there is also formidable resistance, supposedly, from some officials and residents of Wyoming. The resistance should yield to time, patience and effort." So it has yielded to time and Digong.

"The story line at the base is only about the Filipino massacre of the American soldiers. Nothing is said about the My Lai-type reprisal when Gen. Jacob Smith ordered in 1901 every male 10 years or older to be killed and Samar converted into a howling wilderness.

"The bells, like a 16th-century Buddhist temple bell taken by US Marines from Okinawa 45 years ago and returned to Japan in April, 1992, belong in Balangiga (why not replace them with replicas in Warren?) May they ring in freedom there.

"I have compiled some literature on the subject for some years now. I have copies of documents obtained under the Freedom of Information Act (Case No. 9205A) which include letters to Wyoming Senator Alan K. Simpson, opposing the return of the bells and cannon to us; accounts on the `War Trophies from Balangiga P.I.;' reports and dispatches after the battle; articles opposing the return and the like.

"The original dispatches in 1901 right after the battle, in quaint typed uneven reports, make gripping reading even today. However, one could detect some awareness, even resignation, in letters of protest of recent vintage, that someday somehow, the bells will come home where they belong." This is one situation where Digong's astig image has resulted in something positive. He merits praise for making the return happen. Pure praise, nothing toxic.

On the toxicity of marijuana and fentanyl used by the Prez, we cannot take Dr. Sal Panelo's medical bulletin at face value. He may not say Digong is as strong as a horse, not being a horse doctor. Why not a panel of doctors in Cardinal Santos, where apparently Digong goes for check-ups?

For his own good and the good of all his people, 107M rabbits, rejoicing at the return of those lovely bells. But, nothing has been said that I have read or seen about the Falcon cannon. Why?

Digong's tilt to awakened China might also have helped convince the U.S. to return the Bells. So, China, awakened dragon, thank you very very many also, ha ha.

But, China! You may not install military facilities in our territory - AMIN 'TO - under Sec. 25 of Art. XVIII of our Constitution. We can all be Warays, like Digong, who we owe, big-time, for the return of the Bells. Also, China, for its irredentism, compelling the U.S. to stroke and massage us.

My Bedan AB classmate, Ed Ruiz, just reminded me of two Churchillian gems: "A nation that forgets its past has no future" and "an appeaser feeds a crocodile hoping it will eat him last."

Maria Ressa and Leila de Lima, democracy doesn't need appeasers. Keep going, even if it offends the son of a sainted mother.

Saguisag & Associates Lawyers 4045 Bigasan Street, Palanan 1235 Makati Office Nos. (+632) 551-6350/833-4140 Fax No. (+632) 8312276

oooooo

22
KUDOS AND THE `IGNO' PRECEDENT

MTGIF11/23/18
Manila times opinion - opinion@manilatimes.net

55 Novembers ago, to the day (our time), in Dallas, JFK was felled by shots heard round the world. In the summer of 1967, I visited the building where, we are told, Lee Harvey Oswald fired those shots.

50 Novembers ago, also to the day, Harvard, behind Yale, 13-29, rallied in the last 42 seconds and the football game ended 29-all. The Harvard Crimson bannered: "Harvard beats Yale, 29-29." Part of that virtual miracle was Tommy Lee Jones (remember him in The Fugitive?).

The other day, Sherwood "Joe" Bain, my Harvard foster father, reminded me of the feat which he saw in person. He saw service here as a soldier in WWII. He sponsors a scholarship program in Phillips Exeter Academy, whose motto is Non Sibi (not for oneself), named after Ninoy Aquino.

For another virtual miracle, kudos to Prez Digong, San Beda Law homecoming guest speaker this evening in Club Filipino - for making the return of those lovely bells of Balangiga happen. Or about to, if all goes well. Mirabile dictu! - through Santo Rodrigo.

My fellow Maubanin, Fr. Horacio de la Costa, wrote twice in 1957 to Mr. Chip Wards, command historian of the 13th Air Force, on the return of the bells. That year, the Franciscans also wrote to him, pressing the point that a bell was of Franciscan origin. As early as 1911, the U.S. War Department questioned the propriety of taking bells belonging to the Catholic Church. Waray Prof. Rolando O. Borrinaga of UP-Leyte, among many others, has tirelessly campaigned for their return where they belong.

In 1992, Atenean Chuck Medel and I saw those exquisite bells in Fort Warren, just outside of charming Cheyenne, in Crow Creek, and something surged in us. On those bells, the Prez and I are on the same page, but, we may simply be fated hopelessly never to understand each other on human rights. For such rights, to life and dignity, Digong's Mom and I marched together in Davao after Ninoy's salvaging.

Let the freedom bells of Balangiga ring in their rightful home, the Church there of Catholics who Digong occasionally massages, tickles, joshes, jabs, spites or despises. Our heroes' courage and resistance in Balangiga remind me of Churchill in WW II, who inspired his people to fight the Nazis "on the seas and oceans, . . . we shall defend our Island, whatever the cost may be, we shall fight on the beaches, we shall fight on the landing grounds, we shall fight in the fields and in the streets, we shall fight in the hills; we shall never surrender!" And they never did.

And of New York City Mayor Rudy Giuliani, after the 9/11 attack: "Once the leader gives up, then everybody else gives up, and there's no hope. I had to believe and have faith."

Or of patriot Patrick Henry, in 1775: "Is life so dear, or peace so sweet, as to be purchased at the price of chains and slavery? Forbid it, Almighty God! I know not what course others may take; but as for me, give me liberty or give me death!" So boomed Patrick Henry. Prof. Ipe Diño made us, 1955 Mendiola freshmen, memorize Henry's classic inspiring exhortation as a leader, by which I have tried and struggled hard to live.

That was the heart of the Kanos and Brits then, and of the Viet Cong, for centuries. We cannot just capitulate and bow yet again to another colonial master; in pusillanimity, we are past masters. We have had centuries of practice in slavery. But, we do have our heroes of Mactan, Bohol, Balintawak, Balangiga, Bataan and Bessang Pass, not believing "na wala naman tayong magagawa, wala tayong laban." The Palace's perceived stance is so defeatist.

Kudos too to Bedan of the Decade, Super-Executive Secretary Bingbong Medialdea, among those to be honored tonight in Club Filipino. I endorsed majestic magistrate Leo, Bingbong' s pop, to Prez Cory, who named Leo to the Supreme Court (SC). Fruit never falls or rolls far from the tree.

Kudos too to new Bedan Hall of Famer Justice Nick Acosta, son of a good Pasig Judge I appeared before, an authentic WWII veteran and a Knight of Columbus (Nick may be a Columbus of the Night though, wink wink, with Club Filipino' s Kamandag bossman, Obet de Leon; kahit di po likas na mahilig, pag nabarkada kay Obet, muy pillo, lagot).

And certainly, kudos to Bedan Sandiganbayan Associate Justice Mary Ann E. Corpus-Mañalac, Ll.B.'91, for her unanimous ponencia in the case against Imelda Marcos, aka Jane Ryan, who chose this pseudonym in opening her Swiss bank accounts. Macoy's was William Saunders. The Marcoses were ordered to return billions of ill-gotten wealth by the SC on July 15, 2003. There oughta be a law banning humongous "ill-gotteners " from public office, a lacuna in the system.

Courts seldom reconsider so the next arena is the SC - to which none of the three convicting Sandiganbayan Justices can realistically aspire today. There, a mere letter from a Marcos superlawyer could result in a miracle.

Courageous Carmen N. Pedrosa told the story of how poor Imelda was, in the Untold Story of Imelda Marcos (1969). Tibo Mijares, in the Conjugal Dictatorship, wrote that during WWII, citing Y.S. Kwong, Macoy spent "four years . . . as a buy and sell agent." Kwong also narrated that Macoy's ma, Josefa, "was arrested in Arellano High School for having opium and heroin in her possession." Per Kwong, the "family was so poor that it was living from day to day and from hand to mouth." Pages 391-92 (rev. ed. 2017). We see grandiose opulence today, following decades in public office.

But, I do not want to see Jane (90 come July, claiming several ailments, some of which may even be true) - or any other oldie, goodie or baddie, in jail. In Italy and Spain, no jail time for septuagenarians and up (full disclosure: I am 79, and not all that well; if charged with rape, some Ateneo friend may advise me to plead guilty, proudly, at risk though of being convicted instead for lying under oath).

We should apply the humane praxis to all such oldies. Let us equalize benevolence and compassion, not spread suffering and oppression. Be kind to all tigulangs but Manong Johnny (JPE) seems to be too strong for the Igno Aquino treatment (more, below).

Part of a possible deal with Jane is for her to say sorry and pay say a thousand dollars or two to each to the families of the 169 workers buried alive on November 17, 1981 when she capriciously and whimsically rushed the round-the-clock construction of the Film Palace. At least two were only half buried and died slowly hours later. The matter should be exhumed and probed for fair and final compassionate closure.

Shortly after the infliction of martial law in 1972, I had a national security accused, a young man, son of an Air Force officer, plead guilty in December 1972. When Judge Victoriano Savellano pronounced the verdict, I, bewitched, bothered and bewildered, sought leave to approach the bench with the Fiscal. "Your Honor, I think the penalty imposed is below the minimum." He hissed, "why, will you appeal?" I, stupid of me, considered myself told. Humane treatment is from, and for, all, high and low.

Compassion was shown Benigno "Igno" Aquino, Sr., Ninoy's pop, in 1946 by the Supreme Court (SC). Allowed bail for health reasons, he was only in his early 50's. In De la Rama v. People's Court, 77 Phil 461 (1946), citing Igno's case, the SC directed the People's Court to listen to Francisco de la Rama's sickness-based plea in a non-bailable case. Justice Gregorio Perfecto dissented, wanting the SC itself to order the release on bail. A true humanitarian libertarian, Bedan Justice Perfecto, Clase Superior 1905, was the only perfect Justice I know. (The only perfect person I came to know was Dulce, my lovely late mabait wife, OK?)

I am not for slapping Jane publicly a dozen times either, as proposed on November 8 last by the Prez, for crooks. The next day, the Corpus opus. From the Palace, silence. Good. Pero, iba na po talaga ang tinitingnan sa tinititigan. What Jane did for the country, we should not forget, while remembering also what she did TO the country.

In any case, human dignity - priceless, in a society that would be Christian - for Jane Ryan and the rest of us, we have to fight for, particularly for the poorest of the poor, among us.

Like our poor fisherfolk and their kin, in the hundreds of thousands, denied the use of "hulbot- hulbot" or the Modified Danish Seine (MDS) method of fishing, by an arguably administrative overreach in implementing our fishing laws. For the public, denied what the fishermen used to supply, via MDS, the price of fish in our market soars, affecting the quantity, quality and breadth of our food supply, hurting the poorest of the poor the most.

And now even our Exclusive Economic Zone is for China alone to fish in?

Is the Palace pro- or anti-poor?

Saguisag & Associates Lawyers 4045 Bigasan Street, Palanan 1235 Makati Office Nos. (+632) 551-6350/833-4140 Fax No. (+632) 831-2276

oooooo

23
SHOULD JANE RYAN BE SLAPPED PUBLICLY? NO, ABSOLUTELY!

MTGIF11-16-18
Manila times opinion
<opinion@manilatimes.net>

Last Tuesday, San Beda won the NCAA title, for the umpteenth time. One Tisoy alum told me during a break that integrity and delicadeza we had in our time on campus (50's and 60's, when we'd hear stories of rich men entering public life and leaving it poor as well as delicadeza) seem lost and gone forever. He will remain unnamed. TY, Tisoy, for the Islander slippers. But, I can name Senate aspirant Romy Macalintal, with us on the Bedan side; he mentioned an obscure election lawyer somewhere in the huge crowd, a certain Boy Brillantes.

Yup, badly diminished integrity today at a time of our proud and profane Bedan Prez. Our sense of decency eroded when William Saunders (Macoy) and Jane Ryan (Imelda) opened their secret Swiss bank accounts not long after he became Prez in 1965.

Digong says certain grafters should be slapped publicly, in his presence, to strip them of their dignity. This shocking atavistic medieval suggestion he made last November 8. The very next day, Jane was slapped, figuratively. Should she also be slapped literally as a convicted crook?

Absolutely not! Conviction, to me, is humiliating enough. The Sandiganbayan judgment is compatible with the July 15, 2003 Supreme Court (SC) decision mandating the kleptocratic

Marcoses to return billions in ill-gotten wealth. Done. A portion of same was used to compensate human rights claimants under R.A. No. 10368, signed by forgetful Senate Prez Juan Ponce Enrile, among others.

Talk of pardon for Jane is rife, if speculative. Why she and some counsel were absent during the promulgation was not - to my dirty mind - inconsistent with knowing beforehand the verdict in this talkative town of leaks and no secrets. If to be acquitted, she probably would have been present, to preen and luxuriate. Absence, even rookie lawyers in a rinky-dink firm are creative in giving excuses for, some of which may even be true. Wink, wink. Indeed poverty and obscurity may help - the awa factor - while prominence and wealth hurt Jane.

Graft convicts, as a general proposition, all enjoy liberty on bail and can even ran for office until the judgment of conviction becomes, final, unappealable and executory. (I was Cong. Romy Jaloslos' s election lawyer who won reelection twice; his criminal case was handled by eminent respected lawyers).

Imelda will be 90 come July, 2019. In Spain and Italy, no jail time for those aged 70 and above. We should look at these norms - house arrest, community service and other conditions. Countless ordinary poor prisoners should benefit from such a humanitarian arrangement, given our horrid prison conditions the wealthy can avoid. The poor cannot.

In the hypothetical case of Jane, a pardon should be conditioned on say, saying sorry and paying a thousand dollars each to the families of the 169 victims buried alive and entombed in the Film Palace. She had rushed the round-the-clock construction of the structure and on November 17, 1981, her caprice caused the collapse of a fifth floor scaffolding; the quick drying cement killed the trapped workers. I pity in particular the workers who were half buried only; it took hours for them to turn black and blue before giving up the ghost. A probe should help establish what happened in 1981, like how many exactly were killed. Then, closure and talk of restless wandering wailing victims in the Palace in the still of the night would stop.

I hail the Sandiganbayan Division which unanimously ruled against Imelda. The convicting Justices' promotion may be stunted but good to know what the Rule of Law still works from time to time. The Division is chaired by Justice Rafael R. Lagos, No. 1 in the bar exams in 1980, from UP (here, not for Useless People, like Upsilonian William Saunders, a name that can be added to his headstone (AKA). A star prosecution witness against Imelda was the late Frank Chavez, another useful UP Law alum, if a Sigma Rho-gue). The ponente of the 79-page single-spaced Decision was Justice Maryanne E. Corpus-Manalac, concurred in by Chairperson Lagos and Justice Ma. Theresa V. Mendoza-Arcega. Of course some Miracle Workers can still have the decision reversed in the SC but at 90 with health issues, what has the Lord in store for her? A conditional pardon I can live with, for all septuagenarian, octogenarian and nonagenarian prisoners.

And what's in store for us in 2022? Who will be Numero Uno then, Leni Robredo, Grace Poe, Bongbong Marcos, Manny Pacquiao, whoever? Bongbong is damaged goods but one never knows in a country where Top House Absentee contender Manny Pacquiao landed No. 7 in the race for the Senate, where Lito Lapid may return triumphantly in 2019.

Rappler and Maria Ressa are being dunned P108M in taxes, being critical of the Prez. Ultra-smart Manny Pacquiao brown-noses Digong while treating Senate work as a hobby or sideline. No one talks about his case of tax avoidance/evasion in the billions. He intends to fight again Wassisname? in January and then later, Floyd Mayweather. His income should allow him to settle his BIR taxes. A champion tax avoider? Or evader? Is integrity a factor in the Senate he neglects?

Digong misspoke when he said economic adviser Michael Yang is not employed by the government. Documents show otherwise. Michael is Chinese in what otherwise should be an all-Pinoy Civil Service. R.A. No. 6713 requires "nationalism and patriotism" and one should be "loyal to the Republic and to the Filipino people" and "defend Philippine sovereignty against foreign intrusion." Sec. 4(f).

Are the Chinese coming? Or have they in fact been here

since yesteryear? Perry Diaz reminds us that for the past decades, the prospect of Chinese invasion has worried us. In 1994, China claimed the Panganiban Reef, aka as Mischief Reef, in the West Philippine Sea (WPS). It started building artificial islands around seven reefs in the Spratly Islands in the WPS in 2013, following the years of GMA, very cozy with Chinese businessmen.

In May 2017, Digong met Chinese Prez Xi Jinping in Beijing. He boldly told Xi the area was ours. Irredentist Xi threatened war. On February 19, 2018, Digong told Tsinoy businessmen: "If you want, just make us a province, like Fujian." In July 2018, residents in Manila and other cities woke up to see red banners hanging from footbridges reading, "Welcome to the Philippines, province of China."

Chinese gaming companies and tourists have fueled a real estate boom. Due to the demand for facilities, offices and houses by the Chinese expats, property values, to the detriment of homeless Pinoys, have skyrocketed, employing mostly Chinese nationals. Chinese groups use almost quarter of a million square meters of office space. Chinese casino Galaxy Entertainment Group is said to open soon a $550M casino in Boracay (contradicted by recent reports.)

Sen. Leila de Lima filed a resolution urging the Senate to probe the "problem . . . [that] "not only steals jobs away from ordinary Filipinos but also triggers property surge in many developed areas."

Perry Diaz concludes: "Just like 600 years ago when China claimed and placed Luzon under her empire, is she now in a position to claim the Philippines as her province or vassal state? Or has Chinese colonization begun?"

Let's see who we get as the third Telco player. From China? It seems my fellow Bedan, bright Gringo Honasan, is the chosen one for the DICT (Department of Information & Communications Technology]. This is the kind of "voluntary renunciation" that bars him from reelection next year, clearly distinguishable from Senator Koko Pimentel' s "involuntary deprivation" suffered from 2007 to 2011. Anyway, where does Gringo stand on the matter of Yellow Peril? I just signed a petition against the China-financed Kaliwa Dam - another Michael Yang slam-dunk?

No threat is coming from us unabashed Dilawans, the few of us, remaining unreconstructed and unrepentant, who simply do not agree that we prevent rape by giving our timely consent, for money, making us high-class prostitutes. Mejor que nada? Better than nothing? At times, nada es mejor. Nothing is better. So I explained my No! vote on the U.S. bases on September 16, 1991.

Dignity is a priceless human right, even for Jane Ryan.

Saguisag & Associates Lawyers 4045 Bigasan Street, Palanan 1235 Makati Office Nos. (+632) 551-6350/833-4140 Fax No. (+632) 831-2276

oooooooo

24
THE 1972-86 MILITARIZATION

MTGIF11-09-18
To: Manila times opinion
opinion@manilatimes.net

Had Prez Digong attended the first game last Monday of the NCAA Finals between his two alma maters, San Beda and Lyceum, he could have stayed after the final buzzer to join both in singing their respective alma mater songs. Both schools claim him, with San Beda claiming he is from Lyceum which claims he is from San Beda. Seriously, both schools have reason to be proud of him.

And to look askance at his having a Chinese adviser, Michael Yang, for one thing. Yang cannot be expected to comply with Sec. 4(e) of R.A.. No. 6713, to "be loyal to the Republic and to the Filipino people" and "to maintain and defend our sovereignty against foreign intrusion," given China's insatiable irridentism. Now, the Telco bidding with a Tsinoy and pure Chinese winning. . . .

I arrived at the MOA Arena for the second half, with the Red Lions way ahead of the red Pirates, who, with their star, CJ Perez, suspended, predictably lost.

Lyceum offers a course in Customs Administration. I wonder if any soldier has taken it. It might help enable the AFP tell Customs administration from a hole in the ground.

Current Customs chief Ray Leonardo Guerrero may take some time looking for the comfort room - and zone - there. The administration may want to rehire SGS (Societe General de Surveillance) , a true experienced hand in Customs matters. SGS may help train green personnel na pinabili lang po ng suka, Customs Examiner na. But, our 1972-86 experience with the military scares the bejesus out of me. They did not only run Customs, but the entire country, and left a mess.

My darling apo, Dulcet, as pretty and vivacious as her late Lola Dulce, turns eight on Sunday. Last Sunday, we went to Greenbelt for lunch and Mass. Was I pleasantly shocked when she asked me if she could borrow my copy of Raissa Robles's Never Again, whose Foreword I had written. Raissa's best-selling magnum opus should help ensure that our dark past - when our values, institutions and processes took a hit, gone with the wind - won't be soon forgotten, by our children and apos.

Apologists even strangely contend that there were more human rights violations during Cory's watch than in the time of Marcos. Well, I keep retelling here that a Rizal High classmate of mine who attended PMA and landed No. 3 there on graduation, told me about the razing of Jolo on February 7-8, 1974, butchering 20,000 Muslims, et al. Then, there was the September 1974 Malisbong Massacre, when 1,500 Muslim men were killed in a mosque and the women were raped. No free press under the dominative military at the time.

Macoy had to be buried in shame secretly in the Libingan

ng mga Bayani, to fulfill his far from contrite family's sad and needlessly divisive idee fixe. Like a thief in the night he was interred. Ninoy and Cory were buried openly and publicly in Manila Memorial, accompanied by mourning throngs. The standing joke during the dark 1983-86 years was many more might have gone as a hooting throng to the wake of those the people would want to make sure were gone.

The January 22, 1987 Mendiola Massacre? We were at the Guest House that late afternoon monitoring on TV the march led by Ka Jimmy Tadeo. The marchers, to our shock, did not stop for the usual dialogue, forcibly and swiftly breaching the police lines, as agents provocateurs; shots rang out at the back of the marchers, we were told on good authority.

The surprised police and soldiers shot back in our defense in the Palace. Some rallyists were killed, whose remains Ka Senator Tanny Tañada and I viewed in Mt. Carmel Church. I swear that he petulantly told me, "they weren't farmers!" Maybe they were but I know and remember what I am told, even in my Second Adolescence (OK, Childhood). (When the marchers were to return a few days later, I wanted them to turn left on Concepcion Aguila from Mendiola. Tanny said we were "niggardly, extending rights to citizens "begrudgingly, giving them crumbs," and said J.P. Laurel, in front of the Palace. I folded. His wish, my command. Ka Tanny led the march, with Raffy Alunan, Maring Feria, Dick Powell, Lulu Teodoro, Bea Zobel, and Ministers Mita Pardo de Tavera and Joe Concepcion, et al.)

Later that night, another mini-coup occurred as if those day and night incidents were the product of some doomed sinister conspiracy. Defense Minister Rocky Ileto (a West Pointer, who was not sold on, and opposed, martial law and had been banished by Macoy to foreign kangkungans) resigned on January 22, 1987, on the spot, which Prez Coryturned down.. General Mon Montaño manfully took responsibility.

Prez Cory was sued twice on Mendiola, during her term - when I could and did not practice - and after. Both suits were dismissed. The 1999 suit the late Ding Tanjuatco, Dean Mel

Sta. Maria and I handled; it was thrown out by Quezon City Regional Trial Court Judge Percival Mandap Lopez.

Now, the spectre of militarization of the bureaucracy. The police, "civilian in character," per the Constitution (Art. XVI, Sec.. 6), would have been a logical choice to run Customs. But, Digong preferred militarization over "policesizatio n." Digong rejected the police Kotong option, indicating that any time we shake hands with a cop, to be sure to count our fingers afterwards.

But, one military Major General was convicted for filching multimillions and sent to Muntinlupa (where he reportedly reformed and became a lay servant of the Lord; very good). Then there is a Brigadier General, who may have to spend centuries in prison, for the AFP-RSBS (Retirement and Separation Benefits System) scandal. His case is pending in the Sandiganbayan where his motion to reconsider his conviction was denied last month.

When Marcos inflicted martial law, it could not be said that he was unpopular. Few of a busabos-alipin race used to being subjugated for centuries, took the less travelled road and openly resisted. On October 10, 1975, my fellow Maubanin, Fr. Horacio de la Costa, and my Pasig townsman, Uncle Jovy Salonga, sent out a pamphlet, A Message of Hope to Filipinos Who Care, signed by 150 others (including obscure me, focused on human rights violations). Then foreign pressure impelled Macoy to hold trials in the military commissions.

Retired Justice JBL Reyes, liking my maverick articles in the Rizal IBP Chapter Newsletter, invited me to join the Free Legal Assistance Group (FLAG). Earlier, Ka Pepe Diokno was released after two years in detention without being charged! He founded FLAG. Son La Salle Law Dean Chel is running for the Senate. Last Monday, I saw Romy Macalintal watching the SBU-Lyceum game, with a woman he said was the one he had married (without winking, ha). Let's send the two decent men to the Senate.

It was in 1978 when discontent widened with the rigged polls leading to boycotting the 1980 and 1981 "elections. " (On April 6, 1978, an unforgettable noise barrage we had when

Metro Manila exploded in loud peaceful protest all through the night.) Then Ninoy was salvaged in 1983 and galvanized the widening opposition. Edsa'86 made us the world's darlings, a phenomenon that lasted two years. Early in 1988, local elections were held; it has been downhill since.

Thus, I continue to be disturbed by the militarization of Customs, after the military' s Nicanor Faeldon and Sid Lapeña blew it. In fact, the military bungled it when it ran the country from September 1972 to February 1986.

Again, should we not have considered the "policezisatio n of Customs? But, given the recent sorry record of the Pulis Patolas, would the 1972-86 Sundalong Putiks be any better?" As Al Smith would say, "let' s look at the record." Power tends to corrupt and absolute power corrupts absolutely. - Lord Acton.

Our cops and soldiers may need a 9/11 moment, when soldiers and police made the awesome ultimate sacrifice, appreciated by a grateful populace. New York City Mayor Rudolf Giuliani shone and wrote: "We are tied together because we respect human life and the rule of law." Do we, here?

On 9/11/01, when Muslims terrorists attacked and fell the Twin Towers, Rudy, with a priest, checked if anyone was in a church and saw two looters. He barked, "put that fucking stuff down and get out of here," and at once "regretted my language, suddenly remembering that I was in church, next to a priest. But it worked, and the would-be looters dropped them back at the altar and ran out of the church."

He then "turned his attention to my loved ones, to secure wife Donna and kulasisi Judith. Why am I reminded of Congressman-to-be Jojo Binay?" I think "be fruitful and multiply" alluded to children, not partners. A MABINI lawyer was caught in a newspaper pix with arms around a GRO, and was asked by the press: "Is that you, Sir?" The first "I" in MABINI is for integrity, and all he could mumble was, "I' m not sure.

Who will the gods bless on Monday when San Beda again meet Lyceum? I'm not sure, either.

Saguisag & Associates Lawyers 4045 Bigasan Street, Palanan 1235 Makati Office Nos. (+632) 551-6350/833-4140

Fax No. (+632) 831-2276>

oooooo

25
CREEPING MILITARIZATION NOW GALLOPING?

MTGIF11-2-18
Manila times opinion
<opinion@manilatimes.net>

Senator Manny Pacquiao has reportedly been invited by the Oxford Union, which in 1933 voted that "this House [Union] will in no circumstances fight for King and Country," following a similar result in the Cambridge Union in 1927, and arguably giving Hitler aid and comfort.

Muhammad Ali said: "I' m not just a boxer. . . . Even Oxford University, your biggest seat of learning, offered me a Professorship in Philosophy and Poetry to come and teach. I am not just an ordinary fighter, I can talk all week on millions of subjects and you don't have enough wisdom to corner me on television." M. Parkinson, Muhammad Ali: A Memoir 11 (2017) **Spoken by Ali trippingly on the tongue, in England, which > country started in 1956 the world nuke power program for commercial purposes; there a debate on it continues. Scotland has taken the position: no new nuke plants.

Finance Secretary Sonny Dominguez reportedly said that "the government is studying the idea of reviving the Bataan Nuclear Power Plant (BNPP) in a bid to help bring down power rates in the country." Last week, Energy Secretary Alfonso Cusi said the nuke option is high on the list of energy policy-makers, though he stressed they were not necessarily eyeing the BNPP but will more likely pitch for building a new power plant in the country. He said the apprehensions about the security of nuke plants had been raised in the past, and stressed that it was time for us to learn from our neighbors.

Such as Japan? Its Fukushima Daiichi nuke plant had an accident seven years ago and its radioactive water problem continues. Can we, with our puede-na mentality, deal with nuke accidents? Such as Fukushima (2011), Chernobyl (1986) or Three-Mile Island (1979)? Permit me to doubt.

In 1976, Marcos ordered the building of a $2.3-billion nuclear power plant in Morong, Bataan, to diversify our energy source. Energy Secretary Ting Paterno asked why we were paying for one plant at the price of two. The BNPP was completed in 1984, but has failed to produce a single watt of electricity due to public opposition arising from safety concerns.

As Chair of the 1986 Cabinet Committee and the 1987-92 Senate Committee on the Bataan Nuke Plant, I recall that a key conclusion we reached was that the plant was beyond economic repair. Better to build another from the ground up. But where? Well, baby, NIMBY, Not In My Backyard. It was easy for me to push not putting the Bataan nuke plant on line as Chernobyl occurred in April 1986, just weeks after we took power. Deus ex machina.

Admittedly, we do not have the technical expertise and experience of Japan, which has not quite solved the Fukushima problem. Nor the scientific sophistication of the Kanos and the Russkies, with all due respect to our engineers (my late Kuya who attended Mapua was with Bechtel for decades and dealt with nuke waste).

So, who will decide and handle the problem?

"You want things done fast? - Get a military man - PRRD," headlined a paper.

From Customs to TESDA (Technical Education and Skills Development Authority) we find PMAyer Isidro Lapeña promoted, to Cabinet level. There is no evidence against him? Then probe first. We cannot clear someone at the top of the totem pole without some process. Now, the military has taken over Customs in the continuing creeping militarization of our civilian bureaucracy by a seemingly insecure Prez. That he strokes, massages and bribes retired pro-Kano generals with plum positions to deter a coup, is one way to read his continuous singing let-me-call- you-sweetheart to the military-police retirees.

However, it is reported that the AFP owes Meralco close to P10M in unpaid electric bills. Balasubas? And we read that Secretary Cusi is pleading with the privileged military (AFP) to pay. The PNP, the Philippine Coast Guard and the NBI are also deadbeats. You and I, civvies, who may shoot ourselves in the foot, miss a monthly payment to Meralco and we know we're going to hear about it in no time.

The palace cleared Lapeña without due process by not even starting any meaningful and credible investigation but instead praised and promoted him to a Cabinet level position. It is a signal to the Presidential Anti-Crime Commission (PACC, whose legal existence I question; only Congress can create and budget generously a seemingly permanent, not ad hoc, office; it should probe itself first), NBI, PNP, and Ombudsman not to contradict the Palace's position. For some reason, I am reminded of what happened to Office of the Government Corporate Counsel chief Philip Jurado who was hastily sacked without giving him a chance to prove his assertion of graft and corruption by subordinates who had made sumbong to the Prez, who did not bother to get his side of the atory. Fire!Aim!Ready! style of governance. The move in effect disrespected a true hero of Bessang Pass, Desi Jurado, Philip's honorable erpat. Philip has Designer Genes.

Anyway, back to nukes. We can only profit from the opinion of experts from abroad.

Maybe the nuke experts can be borrowed from South Korea, which was rubble and ashes in 1955. But, how it has soared since. The October 22, 2018 issue of TIME even has a two-page spread on "BTS, the most popular boy band in the world." Pp. 44-45. Huh?** I had thought we are the song and dance champ in this part of the world. Teofilo Manalo, a musikero from Orani, Bataan, sired Victoria Manalo in California. She was the first person with Pinoy blood to win not one, but two, Olympic gold medals in 1948, in London, in diving. A two-acre park is named after her in downtown San Francisco. How do you beat one named Victoria(!) na Manalo(!!) pa?

About the time the Bataan plant was built, a similar unit was put up in Korea, for half the price of ours. Two Korean nuclear power plant companies, along with a Russian one, have expressed interest in reviving our mothballed plant but all the figures I see strengthen my conviction that the Bataan nuclear power plant is simply beyond economic repair. It should be dismantled. Or maybe the national penitentiary can move there. Thereby, I hope to see the end of the anomaly of the House and Senate being far apart from each other, which does not conduce to amity and efficiency. Relocated in Morong, Bataan it will be easier for our lawmakers to serve one term in office, and another, in jail.

A great continuing crime or anomaly is the militarization of our bureaucracy. Another retired general heads the Department of Social Welfare & Development (DSWD), which I take personal. My late wife worked there as a social worker/community organizer. in Sapang Palay as a teenager, No. 3 in the board exams, and had her social work degree from UP and her Master's from Boston College. Then back to the Department, which she was appointed to head by Prez Cory Aquino on October 22, 1987, which she didn't accept, and then again By Prez Erap in October 2000, which she did, if ever so briefly. Prez Digong has to stop putting square pegs in round holes and respect careerism and seniority.

Now the military - at this time, creeping, but may soon gallop - will run Customs. But, can soldiers tell customs matters from a hole in the ground?

Digong reigns in a state of lawlessness. A Sokor businessman was murdered right under the nose of PNP chief Bato de la Rosa. Digong ordered ex-Customs intelligence officer Jimmy Guban's arrest (preempting the courts, which order Senator Gordon and Justice Secretary Guevarra have correctly ignored or defied). The Prez cannot order the arrest of anyone unlike when Macoy inflicted martial law in 1972. Gordon and Guevarra are working out an arrangement to put

Guban in the Witness Protection Program, in effect, slapping the Prez.

The current state of lawlessness is in the Palace, which some lawyers are correcting while mouthpiece Sal Panelo is fomenting. Decades ago, Cesar Climaco ran Customs and failed.

When we came home from the U.S. in 1971, the few items we had shipped over, some kin took out and narrated how she had to get countless signatures from various personnel, each one with a drawer where legal tender was dropped. Early this millennium, I had business there. A former student of mine told me about a Friday afternoon practice, of cash in bags being brought in. Good Friday, a weekly ritual, in Customs.

Prosecution and militarization are not the answer to graft. Or not enough. We have to lay down the economic foundation of honesty by giving those concerned pay and perks above the level of temptation and corruption.

It would appear that the narcissistic Prez had not consulted the Cabinet on militarizing Customs. He might have been advised to use the civilian police instead. But, given the PNP's Kotong image, he might have thought soldiers would provide the answer, the sad saga of Cesar Climaco and the PMA cadets in 1962 notwithstanding. They were simply taken to Nautilus, a night club on Roxas Blvd., where the new soldiers - with raging hormones - were naughty, and the girls were loose. Nautilus indeed. Incorruptible Cesar had to give up.

Saguisag & Associates Lawyers 4045 Bigasan Street, Palanan 1235 Makati Office Nos. (+632) 551-6350/833-4140 Fax No. (+632) 831-2276>

oooooo

26
GOODBYE OT, RUN KOKO RUN!

MTGIF10-26-18
Manila times opinion
opinion@manilatimes.net

Good-bye Marcial OT Balgos, another exemplary Compañero/Caballero, of a vanishing breed, an endangered species, who left us last weekend for a better world.

In the mid-90's, he was notified about an oral argument in the Supreme Court. He had long planned to travel with the Missus on that date which he could not cancel (super-takusa din pala gaya ko); he pled with me to do it. We won. Then of late, a challenging case I could not continue handling adequately cuz primarily of my recurring health issues, was endorsed to him, to my relief. Too bad we won't have a happy ending together this time.

He was a partner of superlawyer Che de Santos and Tsikboy Kamandag Nani Perez, as formidable a trio as they come. My first case with Che and OT involved spouses in a sad bitter quarrel. The two were tough but fair adversaries with a flair for elegant and felicitous language. No ad hominems.

The Supreme Court matter was an election case involving feuding candidates from my maternal home province of Quezon. In this regard, no, this Mauban, Quezon native is not running for any post in 2019. Hindi na nga po makalakad ng tuwid, tatakbo pa po?

But, were I to fly with wings of fantasy and run for the Senate next year, and land No. 13, and win my protest after more than four years, and serve for less than two years, and then run again in 2022 and win, may I run once more for the same position in 2028?

My view is yes, Koko Pimentel - whose situation I borrow - may run again. He was denied a full term the first time through no fault of his. Only "VOLUNTARY renunciation of the office for any length of time" it seems to me, may be taken against him. A victim of irregularity in 2007, and wrongly deprived, he should not be punished and disabled further today.. Nothing "voluntary&quo t; the first time, as required under Sec. 4 of Art. VI of the Constitution which says: "No Senator shall serve for more than two consecutive terms. Voluntary renunciation of the office for any length of time shall not be considered as an interruption in the continuity of service for the full term for which he was elected." He did not voluntarily renounce, indeed, he "wuz robbed (to steal from boxing manager Mike Jacobs)," and he struggled and persevered to win. Senator Migs Zubiri graciously gave way. Mindanao is under-represented in the Senate as it is.

Latasa and Aratea, the cases cited by my swashbuckling pal, Ferdie Topacio, it seems to me, are factually distinguishable, from where I sit. They have nothing really to torpedo the candidacy of Koko, whose camp dismisses Ferdie's suit as a nuisance. *Ferdie, balato mo na. O regalo. Kakakasal lang uli ni Koko*, which development Samuel Johnson said represents the triumph of hope over experience.(?)

Seriously, it seems to me the ConCom's concern on August 7, 1986 (please see pages 590-92 of its Record) was to prevent circumvention by a Senator who may renounce his post say months before his second term ends and file a certificate of candidacy for his third consecutive term. Serving as Senator for less than two years is not serving for six years. No voluntary renunciation here by Koko. Involuntary deprivation for more than four years, it was.

Clearly observing and not renouncing his oath, Makati RTC Judge Andres Bartolome Soriano correctly refused to invalidate the amnesty availed of by Senator Sonny Trillanes. I had been concerned; revoking the amnesty may impact on our dozen or so quiet salimpusa clients, enlisted men, save one officer (the lone civilian we represented was not amnestied, but acquitted on a demurrer to evidence, a motion to dismiss after the prosecution rests with the defense not presenting any evidence).

The administration&# 39;s obsession with jailing critics is dead in the water here. For now anyway. There is no assurance of course that Malacañang' s operatives won't continue rattling the bones of a skeleton from which all semblance of life has long departed. But, hatred and persecution of critics can only lead to poor decisions.

May Judge Soriano, an alum of the finest law school in Rockwell, who I met casually in the faculty room of the best law school in Mendiola, continue to follow the star pointed out by St. Thomas More, the king's good servant, but God's first.

More and more, our people resort to prayer, thanks to the administration, which now wants us to withdraw from the International Court and the Inter-Parliamentary Union (through the Better House; the Bigger House has nothing to do with the IPU).

We may yet withdraw from the Universal Declaration of Human Rights. But, human rights are truly universal. The universe should interfere whenever and wherever they are violated. For instance, Saudi Arabian Jamal Ahmad Khashoggi' s body parts were found scattered all over. The world is intervening, and rightly so.

I am reminded of Executive Power by Vince Flynn which has an account of how David (no last name) took four slices of pedophile Iraqi General Hamza's genitals and lopped off his tongue. The book has unsavory references to the Philippines. It mentions a mythical woman President Quirino (a quaint choice of name). It also mentions a General Moro (ditto) of the Philippine army, characterized as a rat taking bribes from the terrorists holding an American family as hostages.

The ill-advised insularization makes us an island entire unto ourselves - John Donne - another big step in the wrong direction.

And then there is the Supreme Court insularizing and insulating itself from interviews by the Judicial and Bar Council.

The Justices prefer making public speeches and attending congressional hearings so unlike during my youth when they were only read, not seen nor heard, as a general proposition. Making sumbong to the Bigger House was the pits. Abysmal. Justice TonyCarp educating us on West Philippine Sea. Celestial.

Back to another final journey home. Regrettably, for me, it is not only OT Balgos leaving this week. Yesterday, Randy Angeles, a friend and neighbor of ours in Pasig, was buried, insulating him from our petty differences and foibles. Such as a South Korean businessman being murdered right under the nose of then PNP Chief Bato de la Rosa in Camp Crame, now>matched by Khashoggi' s departure in the Saudi consulate in Istanbul. Hara kiri crossed Bato's mind but which he dismissed. Masakit.

Now Bato is running for the Senate; can he see beyond his nose? There is hope for the Motherland but those who have given up I can try to understand. Do we now have nationwide martial law (ML)? Can the Prez order the arrest of anyone, a power Macoy exercised after inflicting ML? That power he shared with Defense Secretary Juan Ponce Enrile for a while. But, I am not for jailing Manong Johnny. What I would like our lawmakers to look at is the humanitarian practice in Spain and Italy, no jail time for septuagenarians (such as I; self-serving?), only house arrest and community service.

Saguisag & Associates Lawyers 4045 Bigasan Street, Palanan 1235 Makati Office Nos. (+632) 551-6350/833-4140 Fax No. (+632) 831-227

oooooo

27
Why I Publish/Reprint Books
Tatay Jobo Elizes Self-Publisher

Writings are timeless and they act as mirrors to history. I publish writings as they remain relevant anytime. I have seen a lot of good writings in the internet, in magazines and newspapers. But most writers have only one or two articles and therefore not enough material to be published as a book. And yet, many of them need to be published or archived. There are also writers who write a lot but never publish them. There are also old books with no more prints available. The solution is to publish/reprint. I do this for free because of the print-books-on-demand (POD) system, but the printed or hardcopy is not free The printed book will always be there among your collections or libraries. Not all use the internet. The internet access has its technical problems. I can produce fiction, non-fiction, in color also. My booklist can be seen at   http://tinyurl.com/mj76ccq (copy and paste) Permission had been granted by the author/ authors to print their books under my free self-publishing service. They own copyrights to their works. Interested reader may request free reading of any of my books, articles or essays via online reading or ebook. Just email me. Thank you.

oooooo

www.ingramcontent.com/pod-product-compliance
Lightning Source LLC
Chambersburg PA
CBHW072206280526
45788CB00002B/893